FACING YOUR
DEMONS

Healing Beyond
Narcissistic Family
Relationships

Lisa Sitze

Facing Your Demons
Healing Beyond Narcissistic Family Relationships

Copyright © 2025 by Lisa Sitze

Inspired Legacy Publishing is a division of (DBA) Inspired Legacy, LIC
PO Box 900816
Sandy UT 84090-0816.

This book is not intended as a substitute for the medical advice of physicians. The reader should regularly consult a physician in matters relating to his/her health and particularly with respect to any symptoms that may require diagnosis or medical attention.

Disclaimer: Throughout this book I use examples from the lives of everyday, normal people I have come to know very well, work with as clients, or interact with in some other capacity. However, since our Demons are our own, all names, and certain details have been purposely changed to protect each person individually while still providing the deep storylines from which you as a reader can effectively learn. Just realize that none of the references are in direct relation to any particular person. If you find similarities to someone you know, they will be coincidental only.

ISBN 979-8-9923681-0-9 (paperback)
ISBN 979-8-9923681-1-6 (hardcover)

Printed in the United States of America.

What People Are Saying

"Lisa's candid account of her journey is a true inspiration for those of us raised by narcissists. Her story is heartfelt, relatable, and informative. I highly recommend purchasing this book and joining her on this transformative journey."

—**Madison Frederick,** Best-Selling Author of Untangle the Web of Narcissism

"As someone who has also survived growing up with narcissistic relationships, I have never felt more seen or understood as I have with reading this book.

It is relieving to take back some power after reading this while also feeling even more so like I belong—belong to myself, belong to my world, belong to my hopes, my dreams, and aspirations. Thank you for your vulnerability and your truth."

—**Mercy Morant**

"Determined to break an unpleasant cycle, she perseveres; providing suggested strategies utilized to prevent being defined by the effects of atrocities. She encourages identifying your "Blueprint" to live your full potential, striving daily to become better."

—**Natasha R McCoy,** #1 International Best Selling Author, Speaker, Bible Instructor

"I appreciate Lisa's vulnerability in sharing her story, and the modalities of healing that have worked for her. I especially value her words about Boundaries."
—**Angela M Walters,** PHom

"It was a joy to read your book. I want to go back and do another "Deep Dive" of your book because it has so many beautiful thoughts and tools, and integrates much more psychology than my experience with a therapist."
—**Salena Hamberlin,** Clinical Speech-Language Pathologist and Adjunct Professor at Texas A&M University-Kingsville

"This powerful book offers transformative insights that go beyond narcissistic abuse, empowering readers to take control of their lives, embrace their agency, and create a life of beauty and fulfillment—no matter their past."
—**Michelle Reittinger,** Bipolar Recovery Coach, #1 International Bestselling Author, Speaker, Coach

Dedication

To the one who watched out for me from above
as my guardian angel my entire childhood:
thank you for letting me live my pains, my joys,
my discoveries, and my journey and for guiding me toward
opportunities to learn to live my life, my way.

Table of Contents

"Breaking childhood teachings is never easy, and in essence, they are like white noise that can sometimes stop us from listening to ourselves, or having to listen to ourselves."

—Ramani Durvasula

A Letter to the Reader

I am writing this book for those of you who have disentangled yourselves from the true narcissists in your life to use as a reference while you travel on your own path beyond those often horrific family relationships.

Though I am not writing this book as a step-by-step all-encompassing guide, it still contains effective tools for overcoming trained self-sabotage and self-gaslighting. My ardent desire is that you can reignite the spark of your own built-in power, as have many of my clients whom I helped as a life coach. I am hoping this book will help you recognize you are not alone and that you are capable of living your own authentic life. I want your takeaway to be a recognition of your power!

Because a narcissist is threatened by you making choices outside of their version of right, they hide the fact that you can be an agent for yourself. They hide your agency. Utilizing this power allows you a previously concealed ability to decide what life means to you at its best. You really can learn to become proficient in living without regrets or shame as you realize how to be excited for what life is all about. This power allows you to deliberately choose to act on your own impulses, dreams, and hopes. You really can master how to do this without being pressured into someone else's agenda. **When you learn to be internally motivated by your own authenticity, you learn how to do what is intrinsically right for you.**

Even if my experience is based on being brought up by a parent with Narcissistic Personality Disorder or NPD[1], I know that being married to one, having a narcissistic sibling, or any other form of connection to these bent people can be seriously damaging. This book will help you as well—but it is especially written for children of parents with NPD. Learning about the internal power that is yours and has always belonged to you is a massive step forward. It does, however, take giving yourself enough grace beyond your conditioning to be able to truly change your life. Let's find the amazing person you are at your core.

The Part You Play Starts Within *You*

The hardest part about facing who we are at our core is moving out of the trained view of ourselves that was made through a narcissistic lens. Despite their lies, our authentic truth actually lives within us, however deep. As we dive into our core, we can *unlearn* our toxic parent's views and relearn the amazing truth about who we really have always been.

The focus on wholeness, or self-actualization, that I promote in this book can allow you the freedom to heal from narcissistic abuse. Eventually you can see others with a healthy and loving vulnerability while still being safely authentic. We cannot find lasting happiness by always being self-obsessed. Nor can we find it by completely forgoing who we truly are solely for the benefit of others. It is a balance we must learn.

---

1   Narcissistic Personality Disorder – pattern of grandiosity, need for excessive admiration and lack of empathy. DSM V pg 645

Because this learning was ripped from my childhood, as an adult, I had to learn to balance my personal needs with the needs of others. We can best help others when we are in a healthy place of consciousness where we can make those ongoing micro adjustments as we balance our psyche with the reality we live in.

As you continue to read, I highly suggest that anyone having experienced narcissistic abuse seek therapy from a professional psychologist/psychiatrist as the teachings I have written about in this book will be in partnership with your therapist, not instead of their help. That said, it is time to create a safe space to discover!

Side note:

If you don't understand how I am using particular words, I have created a glossary with definitions at the end for you to reference many of the terms used in the DSM-5, medical world and even a couple I have created.

We Know A Special Kind of Pain

An Introduction – written to those who do or do not know

S omeone once told me, those who know (about living under a narcissist) really know, and those who don't, really don't. We grew up knowing no different. The involvement I had with my mother was nothing like what I was told a mother was supposed to be: a nurturing, loving, caring person who gives unconditional love to her children. My experience was having my independence treated as a fatalistic flaw and portrayed as calculated disobedience. Trying to parse out my normal childhood behavior from the trained thinking that I was "a punishment from a past life"—Yes, my mother actually said that—has made for a lot of soul searching. That particular Demon belief turned into fears that made my life exceedingly difficult for far too long.

From the time I was very small, I heard people say that all mothers are naturally nurturing, but my mother's nurturing consisted of allegedly proving I needed to be beaten by telling me all the ways I was obviously asking for punishment. She said I had "acted like a rebellious teenager from my infancy." She did have to *keep me in line with her demands, after all*, I now think to myself sarcastically.

Because she was my parent, I naturally gravitated toward a need for a deep emotional connection to her that unfortunately became an unhealthy trauma bond.[2] It was the only way I could get my basic needs met. Sadly, rather than being the motherly bond every child needs with a parent, it was more like a cancer in my throat that was so enmeshed, to remove it, I would have to rip out my entire esophagus.

Her twisted psyche developed my self-perception—all I believed, every choice I made, how I reacted to others in my relationships—my everything.

Healing from the trauma of childhood narcissistic abuse has been absolutely grueling. It's likely that those who had even one narcissistic parent know the pain I am talking about. This abuse stemmed directly from the very people we relied upon as infants but who had such an inflated sense of their own self-importance that our worth escaped them. We grew up in an empty void that lacked a parental love the world exemplifies as a given. Our parent's own deep need for excessive attention, admiration and control created their actual lack of empathy for us, their own children.

The jealousy they held against us as babies, who so naturally attracted the notice of everyone around us, pitted them against us long before we were even aware of what it meant to be alive. Instead, we became a Macheavellian means to an end. Primed and molded, we became our narcissistic parent's mirror to fill their emptiness, being put on an unrealistic pedestal. Or, we unwittingly became the antithesis to them as their own self-appointed hero and were punished for existing. Some of us were both.

Other family members experienced my mother's narcissistic traits to a lesser degree, but didn't see all that went on between us behind closed

---

2   Trauma Bonding – the forming of a strong attachment by someone to someone who is causing them harm. Cleveland Clinic: Here's What Trauma Bonding Really Is and How to Recognize the Signs; article March 9, 2023

doors. They often missed how my mother treated me away from public view because she kept much of her subterfuge private.

While having to face her destructive wake, they didn't experience her mind twists to the same degree. For example, simultaneously, she would tell me how special I was, yet shame me into submission, and convince me I deserved it. I grew up being unaware that this treatment by my mother was not true parental love like she suggested. By the time I was ten-years-old, I hated Mother's Day (the holiday that celebrates mothers).

On the surface, and in front of the world, she showed perfect parental interactions. Confusion became my greatest companion as I constantly wondered, "Does she love me? Does she hate me?"

Growing up with a parent who has NPD affects every aspect of our lives, from the way we think and interact to how we express ourselves, and ultimately, our actions. For myself, not knowing another way to parent, I took on many of my mother's parenting styles.

Because the pain caused by these narcissistic parents was often so great, time and again we found temporary solace by giving in to the dictates of our parents, rather than pursuing who we aspired to be.

I grew up with the repeated motto, "If mama ain't happy, ain't no-body happy," and I used this same phrase with my kids. I have since apologized to each of my kids for this and many other actions that I have come to realize were not the way I wanted to parent. This phrase was a big one for me but I now clearly understand that nobody is required to be miserable simply because "mom ain't happy!"

For those of us trained to maintain full cooperation in this one-sided relationship, we were frequently not allowed many of the basic mental, psychological, emotional and sometimes even physical needs. As children, we were required to give our entire lives to satisfy the unachievable demands of our toxic caretaker. We were lied to and led to believe that these distortions were our life source. In other words, we were handed Demons of twisted thoughts on a silver platter, and taught to worship them.

These Demons—our limiting beliefs—ruled our actions long after we were no longer living with our toxic caretaker. Our parents' toxic lies became the limiting beliefs that we lived within and we were naturally lured into becoming these Demons' codependent slaves. We became dependent on them.

"Narcissistic parents are not tuned into their children and the narcissistic parent largely views the child as an object with which to satisfy his or her own needs."
— *Dr. Ramani Durvasula*

My experience written in this book can be a lens, as it were, where you as a reader can see what someone raised by parents with NPD had to endure.

"When we look deep enough into ourselves, we find Demons, those little creatures no one wants to acknowledge are a part of us.
Not only are we familiar with these Demons, when we observe closer, we may find we've prepared them dinner and asked them to stay."
— *Lisa Sitze*

So, What is NPD Anyway?

I was unaware that my mother had a psychological disorder until she was diagnosed with NPD. I didn't know what this diagnosis meant or the depths it went to, the trauma, the neglect, or the Complex Post-traumatic

Stress Disorder (CPTSD)[3] this particular abuse creates until a year into my research—and that was only the beginning of my understanding.

Here is Mayo Clinic's definition of NPD:

"Narcissistic personality disorder is a mental disorder in which people have an inflated sense of their own importance and a deep need for admiration. Those with narcissistic personality disorder believe they're superior to others and have little regard to other people's feelings. But behind this mask of ultra-confidence lies a fragile self-esteem, vulnerable to the slightest criticism."
—*Mayo Clinic NPD literature*

And how does it impact those of us surrounding the person who has this disorder? Well, NPD is often diabolical to the people living in the orbit of one with this malady. To better understand the effects, let's consider the traits of both the person with NPD and the children raised by people with this disorder. You may see patterns you have experienced in your own relationships.

What is the DSM-5?

To help clinicians and researchers have a common language for diagnosing mental disorders, The American Psychiatric Association (APA) published a Diagnostic and Statistical Manual of Mental Disorders (DSM) in 1952. It has since evolved into the DSM-5.

Traits

Because the DSM-5 only contains details of the traits of someone with NPD and doesn't address the effects on those close to them, I am paraphrasing the traits as written in an article by Newport Institute entitled: *How Having a Narcissistic Parent Impacts Young Adult Mental*

---

3   CPTSD – can result from experiencing chronic trauma, such as prolonged child abuse or domestic violence. ClevelandClinic.org CPTSD (Complex PTSD)

Health. This article gives a brief overview of some of the dynamics so we can gain a better understanding of what goes on in these particular relationships.

Signs of a Narcissistic Parent

1. Applying manipulation and scare tactics to exercise control
2. Criticizing, teasing, mocking, and bullying to maintain advantage
3. Gaslighting[4]
4. Intolerance of disobedience
5. Family time gets turned into a focus on them
6. Blaming family members when things don't go their way
7. When their children don't do exactly what they ask, they withdraw their love
8. Lack of compassion for their children or other family members

Effects on Children of Narcissistic Parents

1. Tendencies for people-pleasing
2. Feeling guilty when taking into account their own needs
3. Constantly indecisive and doubting self
4. Persistently blaming self
5. Believing they are not good enough to be loved
6. Struggle with confidence in others and emotional closeness
7. Insecure attachment styles
8. Relationships that are codependent and/or abusive
9. Becoming narcissists themselves

---

4   Gaslighting – to manipulate another person into doubting their perceptions, experiences or understanding of events. APA.org dictionary; gaslight

The Basics of This Book

If you picked up this book because you have a close family member with a formal diagnosis or something about this book's synopsis resonated with you, then we may have more in common than you realize. I am now speaking to all of you who have been brought up feeling trivialized by caretakers who were actually meant to help you learn *your* worth but forced you to prove their worth to the world. This book will help you see that you are not alone.

We know a special kind of pain, one that is, thankfully, not understood by most and still very real. Our lives beyond the narcissistic family abuse we grew up with can actually contain peace, freedom and authenticity. Even if getting there can feel absolutely debilitating, it truly is possible.

Believe it or not, we have a superpower that makes this healing possible, the same one I mentioned before. This same superpower also happens to be in the possession of every other human being on this planet and is still specifically unique to each and every one of us. Our agency is not only a superpower; it is what makes our lives our own. When we utilize our agency to identify what we want to be different in our life, we gain an understanding for how to make the changes we need. It is using our agency that makes it possible to claim back this gift as we address the Demons that are currently running our lives.

This book contains ways to help you:

- Recognize where you're willing to notice your thoughts and actions, while limiting the judgments that show up,
- Take responsibility for those thoughts and actions while still giving yourself grace to make mistakes,
- Recognize and acknowledge your own needs,
- Realize your boundaries for how others interact with you, how you interact with others and even how you interact with yourself, and

- Work towards living your own life on purpose, rather than someone else's life.

All of these will require dedication to your own ideas, thoughts and feelings, which is likely something you have never been allowed to do. This will include balancing your life with those around you, unless, of course, you live on a deserted island.

Each of these lessons has proven invaluable on an ongoing basis for me, and for so many of the clients I work with. But are especially useful for those of us who don't live on a deserted island.

What my mother brainwashed me into thinking was my Achilles heel or my worst problem was in truth my superpower, my armor. I want the same clarity, empowerment and safety for you.

Remember, despite the Demons' lies, our authentic truth actually lives within us, however deep. We must dive into our core to *unlearn* our toxic parent's views and relearn the amazing truth of who we have always been.

It is time to create a safe space to discover!

Facing your demons is the only way any of us can fully heal.
Are you ready?

May this book help guide you to create your life, your way.

Into Undesired Territory

*"In every story, there is a Hero and a Villain. In your story,
you are both. All the bright aspects and all the dark aspects
of your persona orchestrate the melody of your song...
You have to learn to listen not only to what you want
but also to what you are afraid of."*

—C.G.Jung

Delving into who I was under all the masks I felt I must wear created through my training was unmistakably terrifying. Because of my upbringing, my true self, my authenticity, was a place I avoided at all costs. I was having an internal battle between good and evil, like the war described in the Bible, Armageddon, and it felt like the end of everything.

A Personal Armageddon

An individual's personal Armageddon is like a wake-up call. It's the bottoming out that leaves one nowhere else to go but up. It's the coming together of one's traumatic past and present that leads to only two options: make drastic changes or die.

My personal Armageddon happened in March of 1987. I was twenty-two years old with a one-and-a-half-year-old daughter and I woke up. I don't mean I was asleep and woke up. I mean I literally awoke from an emotional blackout.

As I came to, I was sitting in a corner of our tiny Army housing living room in Mannheim, Germany. I found myself holding my knees to my chest, rocking back and forth while sobbing convulsively. I slowly began to notice my toddler's wispy, blonde hair as she stood over me. She was lovingly patting my back. "It's okay, Mommy!" She reassured me. "It's okay!"

My emotions were oozing out, and overwhelming me, despite my lifelong attempts to contain them. I took one look at her concerned, sweet face and similarities between her childhood and mine punched me in the gut.

As a twenty-two-year-old adult, I found myself staring at my own beautiful toddler and seeing my mother in my mind telling me I was the adult in our relationship. I thought, *this time I really am the adult in this mother-daughter relationship.*

My daughter will not have to raise me. . . as I was sanctioned to raise my mother!

As that glimmer of reality began to enter my brain, however, my historic fears of unworthiness, my past failures, and my sense of hopelessness were a screaming cacophony. Even if at that moment they seemed to be harmonizing into one giant lie that my daughter would be better off without me, I refused to knowingly take my daughter's childhood away from her because of my fears.

That left me only one option: make some drastic changes. I had no understanding of what that might look like, let alone how or where to start. I only knew I wanted her to be able to live a true, happy-to-be-alive existence, whatever her experiences in life.

Because I knew that my daughter looked to me at her tender, young age, as I had to my mother for guidance, she needed me to be an example of what it meant to enjoy life. I wanted her to know how amazing she was. More importantly, she needed me to give her the freedom to enjoy her childhood outside of adult concerns.

So, at twenty-two years old, I *began* to make changes. Looking back now I realize that making changes looked more like me growing up in ways I had not been allowed to through my childhood.

Intrinsic Worth

Once I got back from Germany, I tried the "be positive" change. I started by trying to think of all the good days I could think about from my past. I came up blank. So the first decision I made was to find things I could be happy about *today*. That way, I reasoned, tomorrow would have at least one happy memory from my past. Eventually I would create many happy memories I could remember.

However, because I was so weighed down with fear of making decisions, of being wrong, of being a problem, it still took seventeen more years of me working on myself before I even recognized the limiting beliefs that were dictating my life through my thoughts. These Demons told me that I wasn't good enough, that I would never succeed, that my daughter deserved better than anything I could give her. They convinced me that I needed affirmation from others for everything I did and that I needed this affirmation so I could be valuable.

I had never known how to succeed without the acceptance of someone else because I learned, by experience, that my worth was based on whether or not I had value to those around me. My entire life's focus had been me trying to prove how valuable I was to everyone at all times. No wonder any changes I attempted for myself never lasted long. After so many years, I was still not living a life of my own creation, and my attempts had repeatedly fallen short, proving to myself that I was useless on my own. I felt as if I was never going to figure out who I truly was.

This disconnect, my self-worth, didn't become fully clear until a conversation I had with a friend when I was thirty-nine years old. She had been trying to help me see my worth for a couple of years and finally simply started asking me questions. Our conversation went something like this:

"What do you want?" she asked.

"I want to help others."

"Why do you want to help others?"

"Because," I answered honestly, "I want to be valuable."

"What makes you think helping others makes you valuable?" she asked curiously.

"Because it is how I am useful. When I help others, I have a place in society and am valuable."

The conversation continued with my friend trying to explain that I had intrinsic worth which made me valuable. I was speechless. It was unfathomable to me that she didn't understand that my worth was tied to my value, so I tried to reason with her for a while.

Finally she said, "Lisa, nothing anyone can do can take away your worth. Your worth is innate within you and nothing can change that."

When I was finally able to be honest with myself, that conversation became the catalyst for some of my deepest changes.

An Old Soul

You see, my mother had led me to believe that I had an old soul. My mother's definition of an old soul meant that I was more mature than everyone else. She would declare, "Having an old soul means you're special and wise." I grew up believing that my mother was trying to boost my confidence by telling me—starting at the tender age of two— that I was more grown-up than her because I had all this insight. She actually told me I was the adult in our relationship. I didn't know how to "adult" at two.

She would continue on about the blessings of old souls having an inherent knowledge that made life easier for them and how my job was to take care of her as her life was so difficult. This insistence that I was so grown up followed me into my adult life. Without ever being fully allowed to act like a normal child, she gave me unrealistic responsibilities that I didn't have the experience to manage. As an old soul, I was expected to no longer need to act like a child because my wisdom left me with automatic maturity.

The effect? It set me up for a lifetime of failure.

Each time I didn't live up to her impossible definition of being this old soul, I was belittled, or criticized. "I must have done something really horrible in a past life to deserve you!" "You'll never amount to anything other than sweeping floors." "You're_____ fill in the blank!": (too much, too loud, too busy, too lazy, so difficult, etc.) My inability to live up to her unrealistic expectations with my naive mind made for a very disjointed childhood as I attempted to own my mother's old soul version of myself.

My life experiences were very different from what she had told me I was supposed to be able to accomplish. I was not taught how to accept any mistakes I made which left me confused and overwhelmed as I tried to care for my mother's emotions. This responsibility increasingly graduated to outright failure each time she attempted suicide.

First Glimmer of Comprehension

In May of 2019, I was fifty-four when my mother tried to kill herself in one of multiple attempts. While she was in a self-induced coma, and because my stepfather didn't know what else to do at that point, he admitted her into the psychiatric ward at a hospital in North Carolina. During her stay, she was diagnosed with Narcissistic Personality Disorder (NPD). I didn't realize immediately how significant this diagnosis would be for my mental growth until I began researching and learning about its effects on everyone around someone with this psychological disorder. It turned out to be the key that unlocked all the other disconnects in my psyche I had been trying so hard to work through.

As I studied the details of what it actually meant to be the child of a parent with NPD, I started to unravel the tightly bound perplexities of my childhood. I began to see the lies, the misconceptions, the subtle manipulations, and the distractions that, as a narcissist, my mother presented as truths because her psychological needs demanded it. I began to see how these false truths were woven throughout my entire childhood in such a way as to have made them desirable to me. I mean, who wouldn't want to be told they were special, wise, and unique?

My psyche absorbed them all. From a young age, as I repeatedly tried to get that connection that every child yearns for with their mother, I found they were her way—really her only way—of showing me any kind of affection. For the entirety of my childhood and well into my adult years, I had tried to embody what she was asking me to be—that old soul—until that moment in Germany at age twenty-two when I lost the ability to simply cope. I had hidden my life's traumas and my mother's lies away within the dark recesses of my mind so I could be that old soul. Unfortunately, I could no longer contain them, and they spewed out of me like an erupting volcano.

Cleaning up that mess was complicated, to say the least, and more often than not, felt impossible. But I wanted my daughter to have the ability to naturally grow into adulthood, and that meant I had to take charge of my own life. To do that I would have to discover what was continually wresting control of my life away from me. I would eventually find much of my whole self, or my authenticity, far outside of what my mother or anyone else had said about me.

Clarifying Insights

One of my biggest insights came from an experience I had about six months after my mother's official diagnosis.

I stood looking up at the open attic of a home I had just purchased. It was not the typical attic all tucked away where no one could see it, but more like an overhead ledge that ran completely across one wall of my very large living room.

In this five-foot deep, twelve-foot wide open attic lay a staggering number of immense piles appearing to consist of clothes, crumpled up pieces of paper, candy wrappers, and…were those photos sticking out of the mounds? I was confused as to why someone would not only leave their photos behind but store trash so haphazardly in a place clearly visible to anyone who came into the house.

I climbed the unsafe ladder on the left side of the wall very slowly and carefully. Determined to clean this attic, I started with the items that were obviously trash, a half-eaten hamburger from McDonald's, a box of a few hardened fries and lots and lots of Twix wrappers.

That was when I noticed the roaches. I was immediately creeped out. There were so many but they were all incredibly tiny. I worried about unearthing larger ones. As I carefully continued, I finally saw it: one large one. He was too far away to smash, so I continued to consciously remove debris.

This large one seemed to follow me, stopping when I stopped and moving when I moved. I got the oddest sense that he was making sure I was okay. I decided to ignore him and not get too squeamish about the oval-shaped, black, leathery bug watching me with his beady little eyes.

As I continued, I found old toys and gadgets similar to the ones I had when I was a kid. I also saw many of the loose pictures scattered throughout the towering piles. I picked up one of the single pictures, looked at it closely, and my heart skipped a beat.

It was a cute picture of me as a baby. I was a one-year-old dressed for winter, sitting in a box with the word AJAX across the side. The box was in the snow in the front yard of my Nana's house in Nassau, New York. I frantically looked around for some of the other loose pictures and found they were all of my life. It took a while for me to process what I was actually seeing but recognition finally hit me like a light bulb being turned on in a completely black room.

This was my attic! This was my stuff. This was my life and I was the previous tenant who had thoughtlessly piled valuables, memories and trash where everyone could see and judge. It was my mess—and I was the only one who could declutter my attic.

Then I woke up from my dream.

For the next few years, my dream illuminated for me where there was more to me than what my mother and other adults had required me to be. I started seeing where I had been putting my private life on exhibit to gain any kind of people connection. And where I had been trained to hide my authenticity that didn't fit within my mother's or anyone else's psychological agenda.

Broad Acceptance

I eventually came to understand that I would have to personally acknowledge all the parts of myself, the acceptable and the unacceptable. These included my thoughts, my actions, my habits and essentially everything that I saw as me. This progressive acknowledgment led me to realize that neither my childhood training nor society was responsible for my current choices, I was. From there I was able to begin letting go of past beliefs, objectives, and ideas that I personally no longer wanted to believe about myself or my life, no matter who or where they came from.

I had needed to believe or "own" some of them at one time, but too many were no longer useful to me. In fact, most of them were extremely detrimental, like still believing I was my mother's caretaker. She had filled my mind with toxic lies and I was beginning to see and acknowledge them for the detrimental, limiting beliefs they really were. There were so many sides to my healing journey but my dream had helped me realize I could pick one piece at a time to work on. That made it feel possible.

Jung and Philosophies

Since before the dinosaurs,...okay probably not that long ago, but for many centuries, humanity has studied the varying sides of our psyches, including thoughts, words, habits and actions. I have always been interested in philosophy. To wrap my head around my own healing journey, I found myself studying Philosophy, which actually led me to psychology. There seemed to be a plethora of people with ideas for how our minds work. One such discovery was Carl Jung.

Before reading his work, I thought my worth was tied to my value, that being myself was more of a problem than a benefit and that no matter how smart I became, I would never be smart enough. The similarities in the concepts of Jung's shadow piqued my interest, and I began studying how to understand my shadow self.

Let me briefly explain what I learned. In the nineteenth century, Carl Jung, a Swiss psychiatrist and psychoanalyst, coined the term "the shadow self," which led to his theory on shadow work. Jung's concepts seemed to explain me and how I was taught to think about myself.

From the way I understand it, one of Jung's many wonderful ideas is that our shadow self is the true parts of our personality that we don't want to believe about ourselves so we repress them and pretend they don't exist inside of us. Even if we prefer not to believe in those parts of us that we most often want to avoid, Jung suggests we embody our truths with the goal of accepting our whole self because they really are a part of who we are.

Since I had already been working so hard at looking deep into my unlovable self, I felt a kinship to the idea that I should embrace my dark side. However, because I was tired of living the idea that there is a part of me that is evil simply because I'm human, Jung's view felt off to me, and I was inspired to create my own, slightly different, interpretation for myself.

When my friend inspired me to see myself as intrinsically valuable, I started realizing that even though some people may see me as a problem, I could still be a benefit to them, if only to practice patience. This led me to see *everyone* as unique and valuable in some way. This grew to become my purpose as I began changing my lifelong practice of judging others so I could figure out how to be accepted.

Conscious Disconnect

If our shadow self is everything we don't like about ourselves, embodying it means we must incorporate the half of us we see as shameful, guilty or even evil simply because it doesn't fit within society's ideal. It is understandable that we would find it difficult to embody this loathsome and unacceptable side of us. We see it as *us* at our worst.

As I continue my explanation, I will use the term, "Shadow–side" rather than Jung's term "shadow Self" to distinguish the difference between his philosophy and my own interpretation of that side of us.

I see our Shadow–side, rather than being a dark, dense and vile side of who we are, as a vessel, a neutral holding space into which we have carefully, but unconsciously, placed our past unprocessed traumas. Seeing our Shadow–side as neutral can help us have the strength to step out of negative self-judgment because that space really is a part of who we are; our traumas are not.

I feel like the dark and loathsome feeling we get comes from the traumas and also our interpretation of what that space is holding rather than who or what we are ourselves. Because we have to hold them somewhere, and even though we may not be conscious of them, they will stay in that space until we gain the strength and wisdom needed to work through them. Once processed, those traumas will no longer inhabit that space and their effect on us will be less. Our past traumas will always be a part of who we are but I believe by utilizing our agency, we can change our perceptions of them and this will ultimately change how they affect us in the long term.

As we grow in understanding, we can tackle our traumas with more resilience because we are learning better emotional regulation, something that, as children of narcissistic parents, we were rarely allowed to learn.

Emotion regulation[5] can allow us the power to be partially free from the unwanted judgments our traumas incite. We can then be free to continue functioning in the present while addressing those parked traumas at a time of our choosing. One example for me, during meditation, when I have a disruptive thought, it doesn't work to *push* it away, so I acknowledge its presence and sit with it without trying to change it or even to let it go.

Similarly, acknowledging our Shadow–side gives us the distance we need from our mind-blowing disconnects to have the brain space to begin working through our less volatile problems. Once we have gained more experience, or a better understanding of the situation surrounding those more complicated traumas, we can eventually tackle the harder ones.

Masking & Unmasking

I learned early on to present myself only how my mother and others wanted to see me. I got good at watching and repeating only what I saw others do so I could avoid getting it wrong or disappointing anyone. I would also limit my own need to move by bouncing a leg, rubbing my fingers, fiddling with a button or basically any other form of stimming so that I would not be too noticeable. I was putting on a mask to hide my true self so I could fit into what was expected of me.

---

5   Emotion Regulation – the ability of an individual to modulate an emotion or set of emotions. APA.org dictionary; emotion regulation

Since our Shadow-side lives in our unconscious, we create masks to cover those things we don't like about ourselves or what we think others won't like about us. This way we can show the world what we feel will be more acceptable. This result is inauthentic living. By hiding the negative aspects of ourselves behind masks, we become disconnected or dissociated from reality.

When I was seven, my church choir director scheduled me to sing a solo. I was terrified but excited. The anxiety seemed to be winning out as I cried on my bed the night before the performance, fearing that I might anger my mother by messing up the song. Instead of helping me process through this deep fear, my mother decided my solo should be canceled.

She did this without telling me I would no longer have to perform, nor did she comfort me as I cried myself to sleep that night. I simply woke up the next morning and didn't sing. Soon after, any future singing lessons were canceled and my belief became that I was incapable of singing a solo.

I felt my mother was telling me that if I couldn't confidently sing my first solo, I was obviously never going to be able to sing one. No matter how much I believed in my ability to sing or how many times I was told that my voice was beautiful, I dissociated from any idea that I could sing a solo to keep my mother's limited view of my capabilities.

We may initially dissociate from reality when what we see happening in the world is significantly different from what we were taught to believe in our home. As children, we looked to our parents' as god-like and their reality as global truth. As adults, we may now begin to realize that the examples they set often didn't align with many widely held societal views.

Some world views are that all mothers will encourage their children through difficulties, unlike my experience in my example above. Other world views of parents are that they give unconditional love and are more mature than their children.

As we navigate out of the lies we were told, we will begin to change our masks from "only what will make the narcissist look good" to what actually works for us, even if it doesn't work for our parent. We will no longer need to dissociate from the world as a whole, masking to stay safe. When we recognize the gift our Shadow-side can be to our healing process, removing our masks along the way, we will begin to expose our authenticity.

Our struggle with what's in that space is real. Our choice to avoid personalizing ourselves as evil simply because as humans, we have the capacity to do evil things, gives us the power to act in our newly emerging authenticity, rather than delving into evil acts because we feel that is who we are and we have no other choice.

As we start to live in our authenticity, the probability increases that we can look at the traumas and lies filling our Shadow-side. From there we can realistically recognize which were given to us, which parts to take responsibility for, and which we need to park back into our Shadow-side to work through at a time of our own choosing. Each of these choices gives us the ability to temporarily continue functioning, and by acknowledging the existence of those traumas we are parking, they weaken.

Rinse and Repeat

Don't worry about getting it wrong. If we misrepresent any of our traumas, they will resurface and we will have the opportunity to work through them. They don't go away until we work through them fully, which then releases their hold over us, though I've noticed that they do diminish in intensity when we keep trying again and again. Of the re-parked traumas that I did eventually get back to, I found that later they rarely seemed as hard to work through.

As the child of a narcissist, my Shadow-side was filled with toxic behavior that spilled into me from my mother, like lashing out at my kids when I was having a bad day. Her toxic behaviors became mine. Some were *affectionately* given to me, like being an old soul.

As an adult, I held onto the premise of being an old soul by trying to hide any mistakes I made or even might make. For years, when I played online games, I would hide my activity from everyone to keep from being judged because of my limiting belief that video games were what kids played.

Through my healing I learned that I can choose my behaviors, toxic or otherwise. I can let them go or let the toxic ones destroy me by ignoring them. If ignored, any toxic behaviors will destroy me from the inside out because they don't represent who I am, nor who I want to become. I allowed myself to play my online games in front of, first my husband and eventually others once I realized occasionally playing wasn't actually a toxic behavior.

Healing is a process and one that continues because life keeps happening. Sometimes our carefully parked traumas rear their ugly heads at inopportune times, before we are ready. Other times we have traumas we are unable to ever bring ourselves to address. Fairness never had a place in the relationship with our narcissistic parents, so, especially when starting out, we just do our best.

If we consciously or unconsciously forget our traumas, however, they *will* remind us. We will be triggered. All is not lost! Believe it or not, triggers can be helpful if we can learn to see them as simply reminders of issues we have not yet fully worked through. Remember, we can still place them back.

There is more to us than our complicated traumas. Our Shadow-side has a balancing counterpart, our Light-side.

Light-side

Light-side and Shadow-side are not about positive and negative, good and evil, right and wrong. Our Light-side, as I see it, contains both what we see as right and what we see as wrong about ourselves. It is us as a whole person. We are a beautifully complete package.

Light is a great identifier, showing us what is in front of us. Being what allows our physical eyes to work, it provides us the knowledge we need to make decisions about where to walk, what to navigate and how to proceed. More than only our physical eyes, light allows us to see how we can balance our accomplishments with our mistakes.

When we accept our accomplishments and our mistakes with grace, we become more balanced and have the emotional, mental and spiritual strength to deal with how we perceive our traumas. We feel more capable of acknowledging, processing or potentially releasing them.

As we balance both our Light-side with our Shadow-side, we create a clearer connection with our core selves, opening the way for understanding who we are individually and as a whole person. But balancing takes continuous effort.

Equilibrium

A table with two legs will fall over because it cannot adjust for gravity. A three-legged table is more sturdy and will stand alone. As human beings, we learn to be sturdy, standing on only two legs because, from toddlerhood, we master using our muscles. We make micro adjustments to ultimately stay standing and balanced. From there our muscles eventually learn to walk, run, and do so many other activities as we grow, continuing to find that balance. Our equilibrium is simply that—us balancing our opposing forces with the influential bumps in the road that come into our lives. Healing means using micro adjustments to keep balancing both our Light-side with our Shadow-side.

We lean one way or the other throughout our day-to-day activities as we unconsciously balance. When we acknowledge what is authentic for us *on both sides* of our light vs. shadow sides, we will be micro-adjusting our perceptions. Though they once told us how to think, we no longer need our narcissistic parent's opinion to believe what we know is true.

Because our traumas are uniquely ours, we are the only authority who can decide which we work on and which gets stored within our Shadow-side. Creating internal balance means addressing the traumas we have the ability to address, even if they are hard. If we never address our traumas, our Shadow-side gets so full that our equilibrium becomes disrupted and imbalanced despite all our best efforts. I found this out the hard way as I wrote about in my Personal Armageddon.

I wasn't even aware of my Shadow-side at that point. The longer this side of my psyche stayed hidden, the larger and more life-sucking these past traumas had become. I had been taught to protect myself from discovering any unacceptable aspects of who I was by fabricating stories. This is where I needed a protector, and my Demons took on the job. I thought my stories were for making sense of my insufferable actions if anyone called me out on something. Unfortunately, they served only to help me avoid reality at all costs.

Demons

As the title of my book, *Facing Your Demons: Healing Beyond Narcissistic Family Relationships* indicates, those of us who grew up with narcissistic abuse cannot help but have Demons. These Demons are not to be confused with evil fantasy novel creatures—though if we are not careful, they can take on monstrous proportional power over our lives.

I can still feel where the shackles of my childhood Demons kept me tethered to the idea that others had better decision-making skills than I ever could. This limiting belief kept me chained for most of my life. They are also not the beings who sit opposite the Judeo-Christian angels. No, these are something else entirely.

Having been originally thrust upon us, Demons are the metaphor for our limiting beliefs. These beliefs become our bondage and slavery to the dark, life-sucking lies about ourselves and the roles demanded of us. In fact, it is our narcissistic parent's overabundance of unmanaged Demons that spilled over onto us.

Our Demons…became our protectors.

If I was to believe my opinions or decisions mattered as a child, I would have received a lot more verbal or physical abuse from my mother as she attempted to keep me in line. It was usually safer for me to comply than to stand up for myself.

Our limiting belief dialogues become Demons since they stem from our misunderstandings. They are what we tell ourselves to protect us from the confusions we are unwilling or unable to work through. However, far from actually protecting us, they feed our misunderstandings and often lead us to make choices that don't support our authenticity as they simply keep us in what's familiar.

> *"Our brain tries to protect us so it steers us*
> *away from what we think might go wrong."*
> —*Jody Moore, Author of Better Than Happy*

In reality, their familiar lies led us to deflect actual truths. These are some of the lies I often heard my mother say:

- *The Lie:* "You are my punishment from a past life!" *The Truth:* Children are blessings. All children are gifts but in her perspective, I was more of a problem because I was consciously trying to ruin her life.

- *The Lie:* I remember very distinctly the first time I became afraid to explore the world around me. I was three years old and my mother rushed at me screaming, "You need to be beaten once in a while to keep you obedient. I hate doing it but you make it necessary!" I remember these words because she said versions of them repeatedly throughout my growing up. *The Truth:* My normal childlike curiosities were not me being disobedient to hurt her. I was still discovering the world and where I fit in at that age and really, throughout my entire childhood.

- *The Lie:* "You think the world revolves around you! You are so selfish!" This was told to me as fact. She would say this when she was especially frustrated at me for doing something differently than the way she had expected me to do it. It didn't matter that she hadn't explained how she wanted me to do it. I was supposed to simply know, even when I was only three. *The Truth:* Children initially only know their own perspectives so being self-centered was all I was capable of doing at three until I learned to recognize others around me. I wasn't selfish, I was learning.

Through the example of those to whom we looked to for guidance, we ultimately created our own Demons in an attempt to find safety as a respite from overwhelming confusion. We would do this when we experienced a trauma that we didn't understand…so we could attempt to make sense of the limitless, illogical situations and conflicting emotions. Like all humans, we could only make up perceptions that fit our current reality. Yet because our reality was not only immature but also warped by the view of our toxic caretaker, they were not based on *our truths*. They were based on *their lies*.

Deep Dive #1:

This may be a good time to take a moment for yourself and answer these questions, or any of your own that have come up for you. Because a narcissistic parent only saw us as an extension of themselves, we were trained to think like them out of necessity. Our hypervigilance around our toxic caretaker's mood, needs, demands, etc., often made it difficult to have our own thoughts. Let's see if we can learn how to think our own thoughts.

The point of this exercise is to *begin* noticing our thoughts, preferably with limited judgments. Notice them, journal them or maybe even paint something.

1. **Can you notice one thing about your life right now you would like to be different? What are your thoughts about changing it?**

2. **What would your life look like if it was different in the way you wanted it to be different?**

3. **What feelings are showing up as you consider this change being real?**

4. **What safe place can you find to allow yourself these feelings, preferably without judgment?** (a nature area, a safe friend's home, a safe corner where no one else can come into)

5. **Do you know your own perception of your worth? How is this perception helping you? ...harming you?**

As we grow older, our Demons can keep us stuck in our old beliefs because they dismiss any new realities that show up for us. They tell us, "It's unfamiliar and unsafe to make mistakes." So we too often sacrifice any new opportunities because we are afraid they might make us the focus of our narcissistic parent's attention. This likely backfired once we became an adult.

Demons cannot grow in knowledge or understanding so we are disallowed that same gift. By convincing me to avoid the unfamiliar, they would cajole me into believing that I would be kept from any traumas happening again. They would tell me, "Just give in to her. It's safer that way." Though that was not always wrong, holding onto my Demons' beliefs long after my childhood kept me from growing and learning the real truth that I now have the right to live my own life as a conscious adult.

We, they, continue to persuade us that their justifications are the only reality and they have a really important purpose – Don't upset the mother. Demons prefer us to believe that our problems are completely outside of our control.

Our Demons may have served us for our survival, but it is now time to recognize them for what they truly are and take our lives back from that dark abyss we once thought was a life. It is time to make our own choices for how to live the way *we* choose—not ones based on the unrealistic stipulations of these abuse-created Demons.

There is no time frame to master your Demons. Your pace is your own and no one else can tell you how you should do it. Be okay with where you are in your process. Get help or don't. By simply being conscious of them, they will have less power over you as your growing familiarity with them will grant you the ability to manage them instead of letting them control you.

Just like in my dream, I had to start with sorting through the mind clutter created by my Demons and consciously choose which thoughts and actions to keep and which to get rid of—recognizing that there might be a few creepy cockroaches hiding along the way.

Acknowledging Demons

As we experience our life, we progressively gain understanding for how things work. During a trauma, the beliefs we create to make sense of our pain, our sorrow and our negative emotions come from our current understanding. Since perceptions stem from what we believe at the time we created them, they can be difficult to acknowledge as our thoughts, something we have the power to change.

These older beliefs only graduate to Demons when we reject any new information around the memory of a past event. This happens when we try to strictly adhere to only our original understanding. Demons become our protectors from rogue ideas that make no sense to us because we are unfamiliar with what those new ideas would mean for our lives. We learned to be hyperviligant to any changes happening. Once these ideas become distortions of the truth, they can become invisible to us.

Demons are narrow-minded and cannot change or mature. Their rigid understandings will create havoc as our dependence on them dismisses new information each time it shows up. Our Demons take our original beliefs and strategically manipulate them into our psyche as they enmesh them with our narcissistic parent's lies. As we give our Demons our power, they take on a life of their own. Subsequently, our identity is created around them and we will do anything to continue their existence.

When we were disallowed the ability to adjust our understanding as we grew, we became stuck in the wrongness of our actual worth. This imbalance resulted in us being inauthentic and ultimately living in misery as adults.

Over time, our Demons wreak havoc in our world as they keep us prisoners to our original, familiar viewpoints, like my belief that my opinions couldn't possibly matter as much as others. These immutable events build on each other throughout our lives. We begin to get overrun with similar experiences that prove our first impressions were correct, and we hold to those outdated beliefs as truth while we become more comfortable living with our Demons.

However, we survived instead of lived.

If we don't face our Demons, they eventually control our voice, our expressions, our emotions and even our behaviors as if these beliefs are the only truth in existence. Before long, our self-created Demons are running everything, because, well, we aren't!

"The further away we are from our authenticity,
the more we live in misery."
— *Lisa Sitze*

They usually persuade us that our problems are completely outside of our control, and they will take care of us. They are liars, and they keep us from actually living. They tell us, "The world is not safe!" and repeatedly prove it to us.

Proof of Unworthiness

I was in high school when I finally began to suspect my mother's physical outbursts were abusive and decided to listen to the public announcements to "tell someone if you are being abused." The result? After they talked to my charming, attractive, well-spoken mother, I was told by the police, straight to my face, that I had my friends beat me up so I could get my mother in trouble for my horrific bruises. This traumatic event solidified my stuck thinking, temporarily proving to me that my Demons were not wrong. It seemed true that no one would ever listen to or protect me.

> *"Be aware of the voices in your head. Identify them.*
> *Just because you hear it doesn't mean it's your voice saying it.*
> *And just because you think it doesn't mean it's true."*
> —*Toni Sorenson*

Proof of Worthiness

In college, I joined the Reserve Officers' Training Corps (ROTC). Once, at a gathering, the entire Corp was sitting in a large classroom while the leaders handed out awards for excellence. My name was announced, and, completely baffled, I looked around for the person who had my exact name. As those sitting beside me prompted me to get up and head to the front, it finally dawned on me that they were actually calling me, not someone else. I was so unaware that I could deserve an award that I didn't even recognize the acknowledgment.

Proving to ourselves that we are worthy takes time to believe it. My Demons made diving into the abyss that was me, the scariest, most terrifying, most grueling choice I had ever made, but it became the most unexpectedly rewarding and freeing experience as well. For so much of my life, I didn't know how to see myself as anything but broken, because

I couldn't truly see myself as that old soul of which my mother spoke. However, as I began healing, I became increasingly adept at seeing what I did *right* and I continued to discover **that I was not these fixed beliefs**, these errant thoughts or these lies my mother told me when no one else was listening.

A Superpower

There is an antidote to the bondage and slavery of the dark, life-sucking lies of Demons. It is our superpower. Our power was a threat to our narcissistic parent so we were kept from believing in it. Even though it was originally hidden from us, this incredible power was never actually gone.

The time it takes to change the misconceptions about our authentic selves, especially the deeper, more personal beliefs connected to traumas and lies, is completely worth it. You are the only one who can be this agent for yourself. The more I recognized my opinions mattered as much as anyone else's, the more I was able to see my worth to society.

Agency is a superpower that can never be taken away. Because of our agency, every choice we make creates an opportunity for us to make changes, to grow and to evolve. Coupled with knowledge, it can be our most powerful, most redeeming feature. Throughout this book, we will walk together to utilize your most powerful tool.

All of us have Demons lurking in the depths of our being. Believing we can just dismiss them by sheer force of will is hopeful, but not even a little realistic. As crazy as it may sound, just knowing they are there lurking is redeeming in itself. And that gives us ultimate power over them.

When I was eleven, I was happily skipping out of my bedroom which was located next to the living room. I noticed my mother walking to the couch, and I immediately stopped and began acting sad and despondent. My mother told this story for years whenever she thought I was faking my sadness. Fast forward to my current life, and I told this story on a forum for victims of narcissistic abuse.

The reactions were overwhelming. "Your happiness is a threat to the narcissist," "You are safer if the narcissist thinks you are miserable," and "You were automatically protecting yourself by masking your happiness" were some of the responses I received. Looking back on this story, I realize that my Demons were protecting me without me knowing why. Understanding now why I did what I did gives me freedom to let go of the judgments my mother tried to place on me for reacting the way she had actually taught me. My reactions were for my safety, whether either of us knew it or not.

It's redeeming to know that I was correct in my reaction to her presence, and understanding it now gives me freedom to choose my responses whenever I find myself in the presence of a narcissistic person. It's not invisible to my conscious mind anymore.

Is there more to this powerful journey, you ask? Read on, my dear friend. You are not alone.

A Crisis of Accountability

"Life is existence along with a state of mind. So, my existence and expe-rience will change, based upon my state of mind. If I have a good state of mind, my existence is affected, therefore I'll have a good life. If my state of mind is in fear of the unknown, then my existence is going to be shallow, reserved, defensive, protective, blaming others."

—Kirk Duncan

Let me rewind a bit.

False Requirements

When I got pregnant out of wedlock in the fall of 1984, as a fresh-man in college, my mother had a conniption fit. Her incessant badgering to fix my mistake agitated my lifelong Demons into an all-out frenzy. She repeated endlessly, "Your child will be illegitimate and will never be accepted into society! You have to get married before the baby is born, otherwise her entire life will be ruined!" Her frequent harassing phone calls to me felt more like a cat-o'-nine-tails slashing at my psyche rather than concern for mine or my baby's well-being.

My unrealized truth? I had no desire to marry the father of the growing life inside of me. However, to silence my mother's constant bombardments, in March 1985, I did what I had been trained to do: I gave in to her tantrums. I married my first husband in my mother's Methodist church in New Bern, North Carolina. I think she truly believed she was saving me and my unborn child from what she believed were the world's life-destroying judgments. Unfortunately for me, this latest giving in, marrying Peter, turned out to be one of my worst mistakes.

Peter and I met in ROTC at New Mexico State University (NMSU), where he began his long-term career in the US Army. He originally showered me with the attention I felt I so desperately needed. However, he and his father had planned for him to retire after twenty years as an officer. That plan did not include Peter having a family before he had traveled the world. It turned out nothing was going to change his father's well-thought-out intentions for his son's future.

Peter graduated two years before me. He and I had multiple long talks and agreed that he would get a stateside tour first before heading overseas, so I could finish my college degree and afterward we would travel together. I was unaware that his father's opinions were always going to be a part of our decisions and was blindsided when Peter came home in the Fall of 1985 and said, "I applied and have been assigned to Mannheim, Germany."

Unbeknownst to me, and under his father's direction, Peter didn't hesitate to sign up for an overseas tour as his first assignment regardless of the agreement we had made between us as a married couple. At the time I was clueless that he was following his father's council. Since Peter was already assigned to Germany, there was to be no further discussion allowed about this particular arrangement.

His father had convinced him that it was better that he go abroad to serve *without* his family and enjoy his freedom, per their original plan for his life. I was expected to stay behind with our eight-month-old daughter. That meant I would need to be a single parent, figure out my eight-month-old's newly diagnosed Celiac Disease, *and* finish my college degree all on my own. These expectations of me were not within my realm of emotional possibility at that time.

Once again, I felt forced. If I didn't want to be alone, I had to leave behind my hopes of finishing college to fly to Germany with my husband. Even though it was ultimately my choice to go, no matter how hard I tried, I was unable to go with any kind of positive mindset about the matter.

I blamed Peter for getting me pregnant.

I resented him for taking me away from finishing my college degree.

I was discontented having to single handedly unpack all by myself and to understand our daughter's recent Celiac diagnosis, which was practically unheard of at that time while he went to work.

I was especially indignant that he was willing to leave me behind.

So much anger and resentment was built up inside of me because I had been brought up to be obsequious to my mother's every whim for her benefit. Growing up I had not been allowed to feel these feelings, so I again pushed them down. It seemed I was now expected to transfer that *obedience* to my husband's plans. It so overwhelmed my psyche that I was unable to enjoy anything about living in the incredible country of Germany.

Prior to that time, I had believed that I had to be that old soul. Being so wise, all-knowing and enlightened, I thought I was showing great responsibility by doing what was expected of me at all costs, even if it meant, once again, sacrificing everything about my own hopes and dreams. I was bereft of the confidence I needed to make my own decisions if they went against anyone else's suggestions. The accumulation of these, with other forced responsibilities and sacrifices, led to my Personal Armageddon by awakening to me how my lack of confidence was affecting my daughter. I saw her living an eerily similar life to my own, and I wanted to do whatever it took to avoid that for her. I would have to figure out how to make that happen.

Illogical Reasonings

That lack of confidence had led me to not being responsible for my life because my limiting beliefs were that the decisions I made on my own were incompetent. I had been led to believe that only my mother, and then my husband, could make the best decisions for my daughter and our family. Once realizing the impact this influence had on my daughter, I became determined to free her to learn to make decisions for her own life, not ones that I or her father created for her.

I struggled because I had no experience in knowing how to allow mistakes, and it seemed counterintuitive to me at the time. I kept telling myself, *I have very little experience in making my own choices, so how am I supposed to teach her?*

I began to notice that neither my mother nor my husband had ever tried to include my hopes in their decisions and my first attempt became learning to trust in my daughter's intuitive growth process. This in turn led me to trust my own growth process even though I was still unsure how to stop relying on others to make *all* my choices. I only knew that, as her mother, I had to *show* my daughter the kind of example I wanted her to follow.

My daughter's small and simple act of tenderness in exhibiting concern for me was an influential spark that ignited my changes. It eventually proved to be the light I would need to see my Demons in the dark recesses of my psyche. Later, I would learn how to use that light with more efficacy, but that first pinprick was beginning to expand into the abyss of my narcissistic abuse.

Perceptions and Perspectives

To take responsibility for my life, I started with truth, *my truth*. I needed to discover what that was outside of all the stories I'd been told growing up and learn not to continue to change it to match everyone else's stories. Those were their stories and I was learning to have the right to my own story.

I needed to determine how to use my truth to grant freedom to my very young daughter so, while still in her childhood, she could find her own truth. Having my own truth outside of my mother's, and now my husband's, was something I had not previously been allowed. As my perceptions changed, I began noticing where I had been repeatedly "corrected" to see the world only as my mother saw things. I had been taught to feel unsafe to learn things without first getting her approval.

I needed to give my daughter the freedom to feel safe to make mistakes while she was under my care. That way she could ultimately learn how to take responsibility for her own life and in her own way.

Because being wrong for me often meant some form of abuse, allowing my daughter to make her own mistakes was extremely scary. I knew I would not beat *her* for making mistakes but I had no idea, at that time, the extent of the lies I would uncover in myself as I created this reality for her. It was truly terrifying for me, but truth cannot be found in perfectionism, so learning to accept mistakes, I decided, was to be allowed in my new life.

I started finding a deeper part of me, separate from the taught shallowness. The more I skimmed off the top, though, the darker the lies I unearthed. It was often so hard to want to continue. However, as I identified the Demons that were running me, the changes I needed to make became clearer as well.

A huge perception change for me was learning to tell the difference between choices that were actually my responsibilities and choices that were for others to make. I think it made it easier that I had a child who was so young because I learned so much by watching her learn. As I created activities she could eventually master, I began to transpose those lessons into my adult life. It was allowing her to learn rather than forcing her to learn. Follow her lead.

Although I began with asking how I could help my daughter, I slowly became aware that I couldn't help her until I helped myself. Kind of like when we are on a plane and asked to put the mask on ourselves first before we put one on our child. If I didn't learn from my own mistakes, I would continue to be dependent on others to make my life decisions for me, and by example, I would disempower my daughter from learning through her own mistakes.

Steven Covey, in his book, *The Seven Habits of Highly Effective People*, tells one of my favorite example stories that illustrates the vital importance of opening ourselves to that perspective change I was learning.

Covey tells of being on a subway train very early one quiet Sunday morning. Another man got on and brought with him his two children. The man's kids proceeded to terrorize the subway car by yelling, throwing things, and even grabbing people's papers, disturbing the entire peaceful scene. Covey eventually addressed the situation to the father.

"Sir," he said, trying to be polite but frank, "your children are really disturbing a lot of people. I wonder if you couldn't control them a little more?"

The man looked up as if he saw the situation for the first time and softly said, "Oh, you're right. I guess I should do something about it. We just came from the hospital where their mother died about an hour ago. I don't know what to think, and I guess they don't know how to handle it either."

As with Covey, I felt completely justified in blaming the father for not controlling his unruly children. The clarifying piece about their mom dying, however, changed my perspective also, and I felt compassion for the situation of this widower and his newly motherless children. He was still responsible as a parent but I too had dealt with traumatic events that left me temporarily unable to think clearly until I had time to process what had happened while all around me chaos reigned that was technically my responsibility to manage. This widower was still within his first hour of processing a major negative life event, and so were his kids.

Covey's principal lesson in this story hit me pretty hard. It put into one story the concepts I had spent years trying to understand. Having grown up unwittingly with narcissistic abuse, my perceptions were skewed because I learned not to trust myself. I had been believing it was safer to have someone else tell me what to do or what I should feel instead of being willing to make mistakes, adjust and learn to be responsible for my own life. It was easier to blame someone else when problems occurred.

Deep Dive #2:

Let's take a moment to simply ask ourselves a few more questions. When we are raised by a parent with NPD, we will often learn, by example, how to blame others for our problems. We may avoid making mistakes. The abuse we received was not because of who we are, no matter what the narcissist says. When we notice the part we played, giving ourselves grace for actions we did that stemmed from natural reactions to the abuse we received, we can parse out what changes we can make in our lives and what we need to allow to continue…at least for the moment.

Since physical writing has an affect on the wiring of our brain, it can solidify our confusions into something more cohesive. It is my preferred (and suggested) way of processing. However, using any form of creative outlet can be useful as we are each unique. Don't be afraid to experiment. Find what works for you. The point of this exercise is to continue noticing our thoughts.

1. **How do you think about the way others treat you?**
2. **Do you feel they are in the right to treat you that way? Do you feel they are in the wrong to treat you that way?**
3. **What are two ways you see others being treated that you would like to experience yourself?**
4. **What are your thoughts about the control you have to make that happen?**
5. **What is one action you could do that would move in that direction?**

Authenticity[6]

I'm here to tell you that we ultimately have the power to choose w*hat* we do, think, or feel in any given situation. Change only comes after we identify what we actually want to change and figure out what we want to do about it. The ability to be an agent for ourselves is inherent within us, it's permanent. That means, at any time we can change our reactions to be different from our initial, trained response.

I first had to stop believing I was dependent on others to change things for me and take responsibility for my own choices. It took a while for me to learn to distinguish which parts were mine to manage and which I needed to leave for others.

After my Personal Armageddon, my daughter and I left Germany to visit family in the United States. I began my healing journey through much difficulty by learning and making my own mistakes. Because I was staying with my mother, I had to keep my entire process to myself. As I came to terms with the unwanted aspects of myself, I felt like my Shadow-side would engulf me in its darkness every time my mother would berate anything she didn't like about how I was raising my daughter.

I still found it too daunting to wrap my head around the idea that, outside the ones that had been given to me, I had created so many of my own Demons, and I still didn't have the emotional ability to fully comprehend my part in their existence quite yet. That part of my healing journey would have to wait. I did, however, start to notice them, one limiting belief at a time, leaving the others for later. That way they wouldn't swallow me up in my own perceived darkness. They are life-sucking dark mind holes that take us down unless we deal with them.

---

6   Authenticity – a mode of being that humans can achieve by accepting the burden of freedom, choice, and responsibility and the need to construct their own values and meanings in a meaningless universe. APA.org Dictionary; authenticity

Becoming More Conscious

It can sometimes be hard to notice our Demons without being overwhelmed. Addressing them one at a time makes it more bearable. As we practice becoming familiar with them, we are led to become familiar with their lies which can become a strength as we are more capable of making decisions based on reality.

While visiting my mother, I met some people my age who liked to drink. I went with them to a bar but felt instantly uncomfortable as it was located in a neighborhood where I felt very unsafe. I chose not to drink alcohol and was laughed at for being a snob. I don't even remember how I made it home but I spent the next week trying to recover from all the mistakes I was noticing I was making. Once back in Germany, I began making friends with people who did more than drink alcohol.

Many ancient philosophers have taught that there is an order of things for how we learn, grow and progress.

"Watch your thoughts; they become words.
Watch your words; they become actions.
Watch your actions; they become habits.
Watch your habits; they become your character.
Watch your character; it becomes your destiny.
— Lao-Tzu

If we want our lives to be of our own making, which leads to finding our authenticity, then, according to Lao-Tzu, we start with our thoughts because our thoughts will ultimately become our destiny. Our agency gives us the power to choose that destiny. That is why facing our Demons and becoming familiar with their lies is so necessary. When we can see the lies within the dialogues our Demons are telling us, we become increasingly able to create our chosen future.

Unfortunately, familiarity can also be a limitation. Sometimes our familiarity becomes so comfortable that it keeps us from recognizing that something needs to change.

For the longest time, I felt my Demon's lies were "truths" for me to feel shameful about, rather than understand that they were in my power to change. These are the two I noticed first.

- As an old soul, I *had* to do what I was told.

    » "Yes, Mother, I'll marry the father of my child before she is born to *save* her future"–and consequently *your* reputation.

- To connect with others, I always had to succumb to what others deemed as right.

    » "Yes, Peter, I will give up my college degree to let you live your Army dream immediately—and consequently put off my dreams…permanently."

Familiarity is an exceptional tool for noticing what we want and also where we are too comfortable. When we acknowledge our thoughts, one at a time, we can take accountability for our part of our past. This means we are more capable of personally creating that destiny of which Lao-Tzu refers. When we don't acknowledge our thoughts, our past repeats itself, and we act within the same old patterns with which we are too familiar.

A Crisis of Accountability

Originally I couldn't fully see my part in choosing to marry my first husband. And, even though I knew how it happened, I was blind to taking responsibility for the pregnancy that led to my mother insisting I get married. I was completely oblivious to the part I played in leaving my college degree behind to live with my husband in Germany. I didn't feel I had a choice in any of these circumstances. The truths of each were invisible to me.

Because I had never been allowed to experience decisions that weren't given to me, following my own path was so unfamiliar and terrifying. These were each choices I had made, but they were through the guiding lies of my Demons, the ones given to me and the ones I myself had created to feel safe from my mother's wrath.

I eventually figured out that my part had looked like me creating relationships with others, like Peter, who would make decisions for me. I simply acquiesced, giving up my strongest desires, hopes and dreams in favor of Peter's dreams. All that did was lead me to being blind to the imbalance in my psyche. That imbalance culminated in my loss of containment for how I felt about my own lack of respect for my own desires. Basically, it led me to my Personal Armageddon.

Ultimate Power

The complication of others making my life decisions meant that my life patterns never really changed, and I never created my chosen future. Oh, sure, after the wedding, my mother stopped badgering me about my daughter's destitute future, and being in Germany meant I didn't have to take care of my daughter alone, some of the time. Unfortunately, these same circumstances and patterns kept showing up because I wasn't changing them myself. Only the details varied.

The truth is, we are the only ones who can truly make long-lasting changes for ourselves. If someone else adjusts something about our life, the only difference is our current situation. The long-term solution to a problem is not achieved. Getting help, depending on others and taking advice can be useful and often necessary. The value of these depends on how they uplift or tear down our authenticity.

What We Don't Know Can Still Affect Us

While Lao-Tzu suggests that our destiny starts with our thoughts, this power doesn't only work in one direction. Interestingly enough, "the order of things" can also work in reverse. Let me explain.

When I was in my early fifties, I had bilateral hip surgery. I had spent so many years trying not to be a burden, to stay under the radar, to avoid creating more problems for my mother that I felt it my duty, my responsibility, to ignore my needs as much as possible if it meant bothering her and subsequently any others in my life. That particular Demon was so powerful that he had underlings and was like a mob boss within my head.

I had begun to notice that I was less and less willing to do much of anything. I didn't just avoid doing the laundry, washing the dishes, or other chores, I began avoiding doing things I previously had loved to do, like playing with my grandkids. My "old soul" Demon was all over that. I was supposed to "know better," but instead my mind was badgered night and day with my worthlessness, laziness, and disrespect for the needs of my children because I was letting all my responsibilities slide. I thought I was depressed.

My unknown reality? It was a slow, methodical, encroaching pain that crept upon my very essence. It wasn't until I began to have trouble standing up that I finally realized the incredible, growing discomfort coming from my hips was actually abnormal. I was able to take responsibility for my needs and meticulously search for the right doctor which resulted in me getting bilateral hip replacement.

It was the first time I understood so fully that *pain changes people*. It is true that our thoughts can create painful scenarios but it is also true that painful scenarios can seriously influence our thoughts, even when we are unaware of them.

I wasn't lazy after all! I had simply become so familiar with my pain that I couldn't recognize it until it overwhelmed me, and my thoughts had become dark. My hip surgeries changed my life. Over the years following my surgeries and taking only a few years of time-out for pain, I was finally able to continue building the life I had started to create.

I Was Not Who You See

Now that I was living with less pain, the changes I had been attempting to make with myself after my Personal Armageddon skyrocketed. I was better able to recognize where my responsibilities lay for my life, and I began to discover where I could respectfully delegate.

I am no longer that person. I do, however, take full responsibility for the choices I made when I was under the influence of pain, both emotional and physical, but I learned to stop blaming myself for being lazy or worthless.

Noticing our thoughts, our spoken words, and ultimately, our actions allows us to put ourselves in the driver's seat of our destiny. By balancing both our Shadow-side with our Light–Side, we are taking responsibility for our own lives instead of giving our power to others through blame. When we blame our emotions, the world's current issues, or anything else for the part we played, we give away our power to whatever or whomever we focus that blame. In truth, we lose sight of who we are and the beautiful balance of our whole person.

Recognizing Needs

*"When we are no longer able to change our situation,
we are forced to change ourselves."*

—Viktor Frankl

I spent much of my childhood being told that I had everything I needed, but I also spent that same time feeling empty. Whenever I tried to engage with her for affection, I was told something like, "I don't have time right now. Really, Lisa, you are so selfish."

Those of us who grew up with one or more narcissistic parents may have often been denied our childhood needs if they were inconvenient to our parent. Even if we were lucky enough to have a loving person somewhere in our life who provided some of those basic needs, they may have been perceived by the narcissist as a threat and subsequently sabotaged. We were conditioned to determine our worth by whether the narcissist in our life was happy with us or just plain happy at all. It's time we not only look closely at ourselves, allowing for grace, but choose to fulfill those needs that we were denied because we were taught that they were a bother. Only *we* can create that healthier life for ourselves outside of our trained codependence.

Pyramid Climbing

For much of my own healing journey, like Lao Tzu suggests, I was learning to notice my thoughts. The more I noticed my thoughts, the more I became aware of my actual needs and how my Demons were influencing every choice I was making. I was starting to look up, instead of down, on my own proverbial ladder and consciously taking charge of how my day-to-day life was unfolding. The possibility of my daughter having a life she could call her own was finally unfolding.

A couple of years after "my attic cleaning" dream, I discovered something that embodied what I was learning called Maslow's Hierarchy of Needs.

When American psychologist Abraham Maslow was thirty-three years old, he was married and had two children. This made him ineligible for military service at the time WWII broke out. The horrors of the war led Maslow to wonder; "I was awfully curious to find out why I didn't go insane." At this time he began pursuing the newly rising psychological self-actualization[7] theories. The term "self-actualization" would ultimately be the pinnacle of a pyramid Maslow would create, showing the order in which our needs need to be met to reach our full potential.

This hierarchical order of needs reveals the foundation behind our motivation to *level up*, so to speak. As a given level's needs are met, the higher levels become visible. and our core human drive pushes us towards our next level. Though we can choose not to pursue that next level, it is like a personal guide to the needs we can acquire in order to fulfill our miraculous life potential.

Maslow began to see human beings' needs ordered like a five-tier ladder, with the needs at the most bottom level being physical, like food, water and rest. The next three levels, which were also part of what

---

7   Self-actualization – The complete realization of that of which one is capable, involving maximum development of abilities and full involvement in and appreciation for life. APA.org Dictionary; self-actualization

Maslow called basic deficiency needs, were as follows: Safety and Order, like shelter and security; Social like friends and intimate relationships; Ego like prestige and accomplishments.

Today, Maslow's theory is represented as a pyramid with the final level being the apex. This level contains what Maslow called the growth need, or self-actualization. It is a need to reach one's full potential. But, Maslow believed one could not reach this level until the lower needs were met. This hierarchy of needs was Maslow's psychological theory explaining why people are motivated to continue to satisfy the needs at whatever level they find themselves.[8] For example, when deprived of oxygen, someone would forget their need for intimacy because oxygen is at a more basic level need for survival.

His pyramid would show how, only after one's needs are met at a given level will one be motivated as they notice that next level. This pyramid culminates at the apex, or self-actualization.

Our Demons are adept at using our unmet needs to create an ignorance, fear of or an abhorrence of those unsafe, unfamiliar, higher potentials. During my childhood, because my mother couldn't rise above the *Safety and Order* level herself, I was never allowed to either.

Lack of Safety & Order

As I began middle school, I had only attended sixth grade for nine weeks when my mother removed me from the public school system. I had been, for the first time, actually beginning to establish friendships. My mother's reason for pulling me out, "I'm afraid you will break an arm moving from class to class. The hallways are too crazy!" Every time I asked for clarity, I got a different answer. The truth, I realized later, was that she was losing control over me as I gained friendships outside of her influence. My needs weren't important.

---

8 Maslow.com; www.pbs.org (Abraham Maslow)

I was first moved to Holy Ghost Catholic School located across the street from the middle school that I had been previously attending. I wasn't Catholic and I knew nothing about the religion. I could quite literally see the kids at my old school from my new school's homeroom window.

My religion growing up was Methodist, so this was way out of my comfort zone to begin with. It was a bad experience from day one as I was doted over by the only teacher every other student disliked. Not a great place for a new student to be. I had repeatedly told my mother how badly I was treated by the other students, and she ended up moving me eighteen weeks later. My needs, however, were not her reason for moving me; my mother said she didn't like the way one of the secretaries spoke to her.

I was moved to Parkview Baptist Elementary, which had two grades per class through eighth grade. Again, I didn't know a soul or anything about this religion. Once more, I struggled to connect naturally with anyone, but I somehow made friends with the secretary and a few other students.

The next year I was in seventh grade. I was so desperate to be included that all I wanted was to belong to something I had been taught was important. One thing I learned, by my mother's example, was that *important* meant what was popular. I decided I needed to become part of the popular group. I spent every ounce of broken energy trying to fit in with them, hoping to ultimately impress my mother when I told her I belonged to the popular crowd.

My social ineptitude made my attempts rather lame, and I kept trying to find ways I could involve myself in whatever they were doing. I was more interested in being included in the popular kid's activities than I cared about my own personal value. I was also not recognizing the worth of the friends I had made who were outside what I saw as the popular crowd. I had one, albeit broken, focus.

Unfortunately, at that time in my life, my involvement looked more like being a pest. I would follow them around, try to include myself in their conversations, try to play whatever games they were playing and frankly, be an absolute nuisance. They finally decided that I wasn't going to go away, and so they found ways to play tricks on me. That way they could at least have a good laugh. But it didn't seem to matter what they did, I wanted so desperately to be included in their group that I kept coming back.

I would sit near these students and laugh with them, pretending I was part of their conversation. I once asked if I could sit with them on a library field trip. They told me that when we got to the library, I could join them. I was ecstatic! Once there, they found a quiet room and closed the door on my face. When I knocked (I actually knocked), they suggested I wait a bit and they would let me in soon. I remember leaving that door feeling like they would finally let me in their little clique but I would again be disappointed.

Their intolerance of my intrusive actions unfortunately led to much verbal abuse. The teachers kept trying to work with me to stop pestering them, and just be friends with those outside their group but I wouldn't give up seeking involvement in their particular clique.

It finally got bad enough that the principal, two teachers and the secretary brought all the girls from the seventh/eighth-grade class into a single room under the guise of discussing physical maturity, when they were actually addressing tolerance and respect. I was the only girl that hadn't yet physically grown into a woman.

Of myself, I knew that it was aimed at the other girls' verbal abuse but I was unwilling to admit that it was also aimed at my unwillingness to acknowledge the friendships I already had outside this clique because I thought joining the popular group would connect me with my mother when she saw I was *successful*.

Because my mother kept so much of her verbal abuse between us, no one else believed I received this kind of treatment from her. Somehow she flawlessly convinced everyone that I was at the same time both a total screw-up as well as amazing. My similar home life experiences were way too familiar to the way I was being treated at school, and I accepted it as normal. Hence I kept going back, hoping for any acknowledgement from these girls.

According to Maslow's Hierarchy of Needs, I would not be able to reach the next level of the pyramid, "Belonging to a Community" until my needs for "Safety and Order" were satisfied. I was repeatedly told growing up that because all of my basic needs were met, I had everything I needed, and I should just be grateful. But too many of my actual basic needs were not being met at home, like empathy and a healthy connection to my mother, so I tried looking to my community to fill these needs. I was, time and again, sabotaged when I tried to belong to any community outside my mother's influence.

My fragmented relationship with my mother had shaped how I formed relationships with potential friends. It would be many years after these school experiences before I could reach any of the higher levels.

Need Vacuum

If you've ever read the book, "Man's Search for Meaning" by Viktor Frankl, you will recognize a "needs" scarcity from one of the most horrible, awful, unfathomable events in known human history. Briefly, Dr. Frankl was a Jew at the time of WWII. He was imprisoned in three different concentration camps: Theresienstadt, where his father died, Bergen-Belsen, where his mother was exterminated, and Auschwitz, where he lost his wife. He, like so many other families, was the only one in his family to survive. But Frankl's hardships didn't stop there.

Before he was taken prisoner, Dr. Frankl had gotten his doctorate in medicine and another one in psychiatry. Ironically, this was the time that Maslow had begun fleshing out his Hierarchy of Needs. His sole possession was his life's work on paper. It was taken from him. Like many who work in their calling, he did what he did best in his horrid situation: he observed. His new life was the worst situation of everything he was studying. Countless deep, unmet needs were being experienced in Frankl's war-torn population.

If there is ever a situation I could find as an example in which the most basic needs were *not* being met, this is prime. Everything, including dignity, was taken from the Nazi prisoners and they were brought face to face with their own humanity—whether they were ready for it or not. Even Victor and his wife were forced to abort their child before it was born, and later his wife was killed. He literally lost everyone and everything.

When we are deprived long enough of foundational human needs, like food, water and warmth, most of us will have a hard time caring about anything else, including other people, until those needs are met. Dr. Frankl felt appalled at the depths that even he himself was willing to stoop, in order to satisfy his own basic needs for survival. He witnessed many prisoners stealing items from bodies that weren't quite dead.

Once the war ended, the camps were liberated of those prisoners who were miraculously still alive, emaciated and looking like human skeletons, but physically alive nonetheless. The level at which each of the survivors went on to live a functional life was determined by the relationship they had with themselves, and eventually, their perceptions and acceptance of their personal needs leading to their actions during that horrible time. Our need to survive is written within our internal code, and lies deep within us. I would guess that is why it is the bottom of Maslow's pyramid. It is the most basic we can be.

> "...the last of the human freedoms – to choose one's attitude
> in any given set of circumstances, to choose one's own way."
> — *Victor Frankl*

Let's be clear: these former prisoners had not been concerned about the hourly threat of death prior to the war. After it was over, some of them had a grueling struggle to accept their reactions to the immoral situation they lived through as prisoners. Living in such depravity created trauma that stayed with them for the rest of their lives no matter how much they worked on themselves. The only ones who endured what they chose to do to survive while in the camps were those who learned to give themselves grace for their reactions to their incarceration.

We often learn to cope during stressful events but I'm here to tell you it *is* possible to find a balance between trauma and Joy. To be clear, I am not comparing my experience with those from Auschwitz. However, I am just one who is living proof that our need to survive has the ability to eventually transform into thriving after trauma. Many, including Dr. Frankl, have proven this possibility even better than me. The human capacity to survive *with grace* is remarkable!

Learning to Belong

Because from my infancy, I was both my mother's problem and her prodigy, her disjointed view of who I really was manifested itself through every aspect of my psyche. As an adult, I noticed so many nuances, layers and depths about myself that I had to dissect and decide what to do with.

Looking back, I can now see my need to be accepted as I was, my need to be understood, my need to be heard, my need to feel safe instead of perpetually worried about my mother's mood and my need to simply live as a child without her adult concerns. All of these unmet needs had culminated into me becoming dependent on my Demons' directions. Before my meltdown in Germany, I had been trained not to see myself as whole or capable, and that led me to being molded into a ticking time bomb.

I don't think there was a specific time in space when this truth dawned on me. **It was only after my Personal Armageddon that I was able to notice, repeatedly, how my interactions with other people were a reflection of what I thought about myself and how I was trying** to use those interactions to fill my unmet childhood needs in both healthy and unhealthy ways.

The thoughts about myself seemed to create, and then destroy, my connections with others because my Demons kept me in that debilitating cycle. This opened my understanding to realize that I had to create a healthy relationship with myself to be able to have healthy relationships with others despite my Demons' lies that only they could guide me in the truth. My Demons went to all efforts to keep me from identifying that I really *wasn't* all bad without my mother's direction.

Identifiers

One of my most useful tools has become my identifiers. **An identifier is something that exposes a limiting belief for what it is—limiting potential.** It can show us the information we need to make the changes that will benefit us the most. It can also help us recognize when something isn't quite right.

They start to become noticeable as we become more willing to see the limiting beliefs that run us. However, because of our need to keep to what's familiar, we often keep a truthful idea that would expose our limiting belief invisible to our own mind.

One identifier for me was noticing how my limiting beliefs about my ability to make choices for myself was unhealthy. I made this one invisible as a child to stay safe from further abuse. Only after it began affecting my daughter was I able to recognize it. Another one was how my Demons kept me from doing anything that might potentially lead to me making mistakes. There was also noticing how my limiting beliefs devalued my worth.

Identifiers often show up seemingly out of the blue. They are usually something we couldn't see about our life before because the reality was invisible to us as the Demons hid the truth. Our limiting beliefs do just that, limit us. They limit our healing, our experiences, our enjoyment of life, and so much more. When the limiting beliefs I was holding onto got to be too cumbersome and I felt like I was in the dark in my healing journey, I would start to notice these shadows.

When there is a shadow, there is something blocking the light which keeps us from seeing clearly. Light, or truth, that shines in the dark either eliminates or creates a shadow. The truth would distort what our limiting beliefs created as reality. When we see a trauma or problem clearly, we are better able to make decisions about it.

Our Demons may seem real to us but the limits they place on our life are just that, limits. When we understand a situation clearly, we are able to see the steps we need to take so that we can move forward, make changes or simply allow it to exist as it is.

Our eyes work with light, so using that metaphor works here as well. You see, light that shines in the dark either eliminates or creates a shadow. When there is a shadow, that means there is something blocking the light, keeping us from seeing it clearly. When we see a trauma clearly we can better decide what to do with it, how we want to address it or whether we want to process it. A fully understood identifier is like an epiphany on steroids. It is understanding with perfect clarity where we learn lessons from our traumas and how we can live through them.

Identifiers are not triggers, though triggers often show us where there is an identifier.

They help us see our Demons that have been invisible to us, so that we can decide for ourselves what to do with particular limiting beliefs that are keeping us stuck. For me, many of my identifiers have uncovered unmet needs created through my past traumas. My traumas were or became hidden when I was not allowed to process through my feelings about them. This left me to make up stories so I could make sense of them.

Once I acknowledged them, it became possible to create a much better outcome for myself.

"Experiences once bereft of the sting of our Demons protective comments, that are based on old or twisted beliefs, become information from which intentional actions can be made."
— Lisa Sitze

Some identifiers I figured out as soon as I noticed them, like when I realized I was unknowingly creating the same path for my daughter that my mother had created for me. Others took years for me to contemplate, ponder and journal about, like understanding my worth.

Some limiting beliefs that are still running my life, I've yet to figure out.

Taking back control of our lives means being vulnerable enough with ourselves to face our fears and our doubts and looking at the parts of us we have been disallowed or unable to look at before. As we notice our undesirable circumstances and take responsibility for our part, we can discover the reason an identifier exists.

Deep Dive #3:

Once again, take some time to reflect on noticing details about your own life right now. The needs of the narcissistic parent take precedence over their children, no matter how small. Recognizing the natural needs we had as children but being brought up to believe they were a nuisance, is a huge step in our healing journey.

These questions are ideas to inspire you to ask your own. The questions you ask yourself will be the best ones for you. Write what comes up, paint your ideas, sculpt your thoughts or simply talk out loud to a tree. Whatever direction you find to use, find what works for you by trying different methods.

1. **What is one need you feel you are not getting right now? Pick one for now.**

2. **What is standing in the way of you getting that need met?**
3. **What changes would help you feel that need was being met?**
4. **Who do you believe you need to help most? How are you meeting their needs?**
5. **Who has the most responsibility for meeting your needs?**

Self-Actualization

As we climb our pyramid, we will find another of our deepest needs as humans is the need for significance. Validation is the one thing someone with NPD is constantly seeking, using us to fill that need. The thing is, that will never happen for them when their validation only comes from outside themselves. Here again, to be psychologically healthy, we need to balance our thoughts about ourselves and what others think about us. When we are honest, what others think affects us. Narcissists cannot truly validate themselves, so they cannot validate others.

Beginning to see my needs without judgment took many years of practice. Because my Shadow–side was chock full of how I failed to react correctly to my traumas, my Demons would enthusiastically point out these unmistakable failures. I was constantly having to deal with my abundance of unmet needs. I often felt that if I looked up the word 'failure' in the dictionary, I would see my picture.

But I was also beginning to see many successful reactions to my traumas, some of which I did not recognize as successes until much later. Having grown up surrounded by false beliefs—misconceptions about myself and what powers I actually held—I discovered I would fall down or climb up the pyramid. These would be directly proportional to how strongly I felt about my capabilities or my limitations. Acknowledging my needs, while trying not to judge them, was difficult but absolutely foundational for my healing journey.

My "attic cleaning" dream helped me to discover that, as a teenager, I ate way too many unhealthy foods because I was told anything healthy was gross. I drank alcohol to fit in. I slept around to feel accepted and desired by others. And both my mother and my Demons continuously convinced me that I was wired to act that way, leaving me to believe that truth meant there was nothing I could do to change. I was doomed.

These unhealthy choices were often used to pile even more negative judgments that I was to believe about myself, rather than lessons for learning what I wanted to change about my life. More times than I care to admit, because I felt incessantly misunderstood, I would lash out at anyone unlucky enough to be near me and blame them for "deserving it."

As we recognize the unmet survival needs from our narcissistic abuse, we can begin to ascertain how to fulfill them at the current time. This in turn can bring us to discern that we are whole, even if this realization takes a while.

Intrinsic Blueprint

The truth is, we really are whole. We always have been, but logically knowing that and feeling that are two different realities, especially when we were raised to believe we were insignificant. It is a common dissociation within trauma.

Inside every human, I believe we have something I call an Intrinsic Blueprint. It is a foundational base for our full potential. As our individual foundation, and because it is unique to us, it gives us the ability to make our own changes that work for us. It is like an outline of who we are at our highest and best self. We get to utilize it any way we decide.

Because we all have a unique design within us, no two blueprints are exactly the same. They cannot be built upon by anyone but us nor can they be destroyed. We can be convinced to make changes on it or ignore it but only we can work on it.

We use this Intrinsic Blueprint whether we know about it or not. It is simply a blueprint that gives us some details but doesn't tell the full story of our lives. That is for us to determine as we utilize our gift of agency.

When we are not living from our core foundation, we feel uncomfortable, distressed, unsettled, confused, and many other negative feelings. Basically, we are miserable. That's not to say these feelings are always about us not living our authenticity. They *are* a part of living a life, however, our Intrinsic Blueprint is our framework for *our* life purpose.

Consciously discovering it opens us up to possibilities we never before imagined. Not our "must dos," or "have to dos" but our potential. It can also show us how our personal Demons are operating our thoughts. What the Demons are saying will *never* match our blueprint because they are limits—limiting beliefs—on that potential.

When we are living under our Demons' tutelage, we will never feel whole or complete. Our Intrinsic Blueprint allows us to shine our personal light into the dark spaces of our mind as its light identifies the Demons that keep us stuck. By utilizing our blueprint, we can consciously figure out how to live our own creative, meaningful lives. Fighting it is like fighting ourselves as we let our Demons infect our choices while we react the way we were trained.

Discovering our Intrinsic Blueprint will lead to the truth that we are a valuable miracle despite the abuse we have endured at the hands of a toxic caretaker. The myriad of doubts that are sure to show up along this path are ultimately no match against our Intrinsic Blueprint as we learn to hold fast to its clarity. If all we do is recognize our need to take back our life, that simple act will play an important role in fighting our personal Demons.

Influence Is
a Fickle Thing

*"At all times and under all circumstances, I have
the power to transform the quality of my life!"*

—**Werner Erhard**

The Influence of Living

Take a moment and think about all the influences in your life...real, actual influences that have shaped your thoughts, your emotions, and your actions throughout the years. These can be helpful or harmful influences. You can reflect on them, sculpt them or journal them. I promise I won't sneak a read at what you write.

Can you keep it to just five? Probably not.

When I originally started writing this chapter, I thought I would talk about a few of the influences that can affect us, so I began brainstorming: society, culture, community, language, social status, knowledge, education, affluence, poverty, experiences, comfort level, our past, stories, propaganda, career, art, music, media, gossip, pain (any kind), mental health, physical health, family, friends, allergies, support, preferences...

I quickly realized this would be a never-ending list.

In fact, the more I thought about how influences affect our lives, the more I realized that there is no area in our lives where we are not influenced…somehow. The level at which an influence has on us is dependent upon how, or if, we internalize it. For the sake of making this a single book rather than volumes, I will speak to only a few.

Influences are so prevalent in our lives that they affect how we develop, behave and think. Our thoughts and actions alone are often neutral. How we perceive them, however, can have an effect long after a particular situation has changed or is no longer a part of our lives. Influences shape our perspective on life, the universe and, well, everything. Every influence in our lives, past, present or future, creates thoughts, and the thoughts that we pursue, shape our lives.

As you can see from the incomplete list above, there are a multitude of influences that impact us. Each of them affects us in different ways, never mind the varying levels of combinations. There are so many that sometimes it can be difficult to see what influences are acting upon us at any given time. Being able to recognize even some of these influences, however, gives us power over how they shape our lives, like when I realized many things my mother did were actually abusive.

Agency, our superpower, allows us to investigate the influences we notice so *we* can determine what actions we will take because those actions will ultimately determine our destiny.

The Powers That Be

Acording to the US Census Bureau[9], at the time this book was printed, there were over 8.0 billion people on this planet. These include our school teachers, governmental leaders, and our parents. These authority figures influence us for our entire lives. Our authoritative caretakers, according to our young child's mind, were the experts on, well, everything.

---

9   World population clock – https://www.census.gov/popclock/world

Childhood was when our minds were most pliable, and our parents held a negative influence over us that lasted long after we left our childhood home. In fact, their influence may still be so entwined with our psyche that it is difficult to parse out where our narcissistic parents end, and we begin.

In truth, I would argue that the ideal parental authority is an obligation for stewardship over the well-being of their children, not an invitation to promote their agenda with us paying the price. I feel that way about all authority positions and that they are, or should be, stewards.

Being born to parents with NPD, we internalized their lies, falsehoods and manipulations as universal truths. They were the experts after all. Unfortunately, their toxic parenting created Demons for us that placed limits on our thoughts, and we were blind to their effect.

Because it was all we knew, the familiarity of our toxic parent's Demons became ours as we internalized the limiting beliefs. The limits placed on us gave us no options for becoming anything other than what they directed us to become. In fact, it was so familiar, we may still find it difficult to parse out our Demons from theirs. As we become aware of the limits that were placed on us, however, the Demons' negative influences can lessen.

Maybe we still acknowledge our parent's previous authoritative position over us, but let me make it clear: there is no reality where we are obligated to continue subjecting ourselves to their abuse into adulthood. I feel that any authorities that have power over another's life never has the right to abuse that power simply because they are in charge.

Despite what the narcissist in our life says, our only responsibility to them is to act according to the situation, never to be their slave. This has multiple levels so from here on, I will speak solely to the situation where we are adults, have moved away from the narcissistic parent and are now learning to create a life of our own, but still feel the negative influences of their toxic behavior.

Stewardship and Familiarity

Let's first speak about stewardship. I would like to define stewardship as watching over something or someone. In the case of my Personal Armageddon story, my stewardship was for my child. The ideal parental stewardship would not be controlling but instead guiding. That way, a child can use that direction to navigate their emotions, social interactions, and desires as they grow to become autonomous adults. I see that a parent's responsibility is to set boundaries while still allowing their charge to learn to govern themselves.

Since a parent with NPD cannot see their child as anything other than an extension of themselves, their parenting becomes abusive as they limit their child's autonomy in the name of protecting them. This kind of abusive parenting sets the child up to embody limiting patterns that get carried into adulthood. When one never gets to learn from their own mistakes in a safe environment, they never learn how to act with their own intention. Their acts become ones to keep them safe from the abuse, whether realized or not.

Because we internalized these limiting patterns, they became familiar reactions to events as they showed up in our lives. Our brains like to stick with what is familiar and our Demons will help keep us stuck, acting in whatever fashion we were trained simply because it is familiar.

If we attempt to make changes, we may worry we will lose control until we give our Demons back the power to run our lives in the way we find most familiar. "Familiarity is safe," our Demons may cajole. Being unaware of how my past had been influencing my young adult life, I was afraid to step outside the familiar. That left me trapped in an unseen cycle of limiting choices, one leading to another in a downward spiral.

Soon after my Personal Armageddon, I awkwardly attempted to make changes that would allow my daughter the freedom to make her own choices. I began to notice where I was influencing her and tried to make the changes that would free her from becoming limited to my acceptance of her actions.

It was through this process that I noticed my first identifier.

Standing on the sidewalk of my daughter's daycare center, I had the epiphany that the problems I was trying to solve in raising her were often the result of my actions and that I was the actual creator of many of them.

Unfortunately, it still took me another five years to discern that, after I left my childhood home, I had actually had options.

This realization brought me to my next epiphany:

Hey wait, that means I can stop causing my own problems!

My childhood Demons were so influential as to completely block my understanding of who was really in charge of my life until this realization. The fact that it took me until I was in college to figure that out influenced how difficult it was for me to acknowledge my insecurities about this identifier. A big part of me wanted it to stay hidden.

I really didn't want to face my own negative past choices but my Personal Armageddon made it clear, it was time I became my own authority if I wanted to be that example for my daughter. The only way to become my own authority was to take the next step and acknowledge the past choices I had made that were now limiting me. As an actual adult, it was time for me to take actions that would create a continued awareness for myself that would hopefully be the example from which I wanted my daughter to learn.

> *"Setting an example is not the main means*
> *of influencing another, it is the only means."*
> — *Albert Einstein*

The School Bully

In the summer of 1978, at the age of thirteen, I was finally no longer the only one from my class that had not physically matured. I even changed my hairstyle. That next school year I again attended Parkview Baptist Elementary, this time for eighth grade. I was quite an emotional wreck at that point in my life. However, I went there determined not to have a repeat of my seventh grade year where I was the pitiful wannabe. I looked so different that on the first day I was actually approached by one of the girls from the previous year's popular clique that I had mercilessly pestered. She asked my name believing I was a new student. I kept wondering what trick was about to be played on me but she truly hadn't recognized me.

That school year proved to be an opposite experience for me from my previous year. I didn't join their clique. Instead, I made my own. I finally took the advice of the school adults and hung out with my own gang. Unfortunately, my internalizing the patterns of bullying, first from my mother and then my previous year's experiences, became my go-to. I took on my previous year's negative experiences of being bullied, and it influenced my leadership more than did the directions of the school staff.

A young man I will call Paul tried to be a part of my group like I had tried to join the popular group the previous year. I began to play some of the same tricks on him that were played on me. Fairly quickly, I got called out by my secretary friend who pulled me aside and reminded me of what I had gone through the year before. I was so familiar with these behaviors I didn't recognize the wrongness until she pointed it out to me.

I have no memory of what happened after that point. I have since wished I could apologize to that young man for the way I treated him. I was so imbalanced in myself, and transferred my suffering to him. It would take a long time for me to forgive myself.

We use our agency whether we are aware of it or not. We are constantly making choices. Our abuse may lead us to do what we were told we had to do or to avoid what we don't want to do. I feel grateful that I had some authorities in my life at that time who were willing to lovingly point out what I was doing to Paul. I did use my agency to stop my abusive actions. Agency gave me the power to be abusive. It also gave me the power to stop my abusive behavior.

It is *the* power that makes us who we are as individuals. It gives us meaning and purpose and the ability to define who we are for ourselves.

Without agency, we could *only* live as we were told while we followed the dictates of others. Any individual growth would be impossible. It is the first thing a narcissist will squash to gain control. We really are our own best authority. The best news is that it is possible to change how influences affect us.

Righteous Judgment

Nelson Mandela was a powerful activist for that kind of change. He was a South African activist against apartheid. Apartheid was put into law to segregate whites and nonwhites, with the minority whites having more rights. It was considered a way to *control* the black population. Mandela felt compelled to lead a campaign to sabotage the South African government. He was arrested and sentenced to life in prison. He was released by F.W. de Klerk, then South African State president, on February 11, 1990 after twenty-seven years of incarceration.

> *"No one truly knows a nation until one has been inside its jails. A nation should not be judged by how it treats its highest citizens, but its lowest ones."*
> — *Nelson Mandela*

Once free, Mandela was asked how he felt about his captors. He said, "Resentment is like drinking poison and hoping it will kill your enemies." After becoming the first black South African President and in an unexpected action, he actually kept some of the previous white leaders in his cabinet. Mandela went from a triumphant liberation leader to a successful political leader. He was a strong man with great wisdom to be able to do that successfully. Just like me, Mandela believed that humans have an innate inclination toward love and compassion, and that these constructive emotions are more ingrained than destructive

71

feelings like malice or hatred. He said, "Love comes more naturally to the human heart than its opposite."

"I have fought against white domination, and I have fought against black domination. I have cherished the ideal of a democratic and free society in which all persons live together in harmony and with equal opportunities. It is an ideal which I hope to live for and to achieve. But if needs be, it is an ideal for which I am prepared to die."
— *Nelson Mandela*

Rather than follow the example of the political dictatorship, Mandela chose to promote peace and equality for everyone, yes, everyone. It was rather unexpected once he gained political power. He chose to break that link of domination, becoming a steward over his country rather than continuing the path of the previous ruling class.

Influences, For Good or Bad

As I mentioned previously, up until junior high, I had no idea that the way my mother treated me was abusive. It was all I had ever known. She trained me to cater to her needs and forgo mine. As I grew, the resentment grew within me, and I slowly became bitter and negative. It took me most of a lifetime to recognize enough discrepancies between what I was taught to believe I *should* feel and the genuine feelings that were beginning to emerge. As I discovered my feelings, it became possible for me to make the changes I needed to make in order to become my own authority rather than giving up my needs to cater to, first my mother and then to everyone else, as I was taught.

It was easier to never hope for anything that I wasn't given permission for by my mother, and ultimately by someone else. My Personal Armageddon's influence was a pivotal point in my life that created an awareness I had previously been unable or unwilling to notice. Even with this newer awareness, I felt I was unable to live my own dreams but I wanted to be a better influence for my daughter.

This event made clear the choice I had to make; I could continue to live knowing things would only get harder for her to realize her dreams or I could make unfamiliar changes to become the steward in her life who creates something better for us both. I struggled but emerged with oh so much better circumstances, even if they were unexpected.

It's not just us as individuals, sometimes the world gets stuck in limiting beliefs.

The Influence of Limiting Barriers

In the 1950s, the prevailing belief among many in the medical and athletic communities was that running a mile in under four minutes was impossible and dangerous to one's health. The media promoted this belief and the world collectively believed this until...

...Roger Bannister ran a mile in under four minutes on May 6, 1954.[10] Once he achieved it other people began to run a mile in under four minutes. It was an emotional release of what was possible for the entire world.

My personal barrier was not even seeing my life's influences let alone believing I could make choices to do anything about them. After becoming a parent however, the deeper I looked within myself, the more I was able to see the influences in my own life and take responsibility for the choices I made in response to them. This became easier when I stopped blaming others for my circumstances and started simply observing my situations.

It became my main goal to see my part in the negative *and* positive circumstances while learning not to blame others *or* myself. No blame

---

10   Roger Bannister and the 4 minute mile

here. I still held others responsible for what was theirs but I was learning to stop feeling that I was hopeless because my humanness made it impossible to keep from making an overwhelming amount of mistakes. When I learned to give myself grace for my shortcomings, far from being debilitating, it became incredibly freeing. I began to break free from the tyranny of my Demons.

Because I saw that my power lay where I made *my* choices, it freed me to realize how I could positively influence both my daughter's future and also my own future outcomes, even when others created problems that influenced me personally. When we utilize our agency with integrity, we can't help but notice agency in others. By changing my actions I was able to positively affect my daughter's life direction. The rest would be up to her.

Pain is a Huge Influencer

Pain changes people and can be one of our biggest influencers. I wasn't consciously aware of my hip pain until I was fifty-one. At that time in my life, the thing I struggled with the most was anger. No matter how hard I tried, I couldn't seem to find a way to not be angry, even for a little while. It was about that time I started becoming aware that my anger was being influenced by the constant, intrusive worsening pain stemming from my degrading hips. Pain was influencing me outside of my conscious awareness.

I had been born with hip dysplasia, which for me, meant that I was born with both of my hips dislocated, and I ended up spending the first year of my life in leg braces. My mother enjoyed having me wear dresses to cover up the unsightly braces. But the metal tore up the dresses even though I was not walking yet. My mother would bring up this story many times insinuating that it was my fault for wiggling too much, ruining the dresses after wearing them once. For my part, and despite the metal wrapped around my baby legs, my body used all that wiggling to strengthen my muscles and adapt to the circumstances. It's awesome how bodies do that! I was able to walk and run normally.

As an adult, however, the pain had become so intense that it was a daily task just to stand up, let alone walk or do anything. I had my left hip replaced in Nov of 2017 and the right hip in Jan of 2018. After my first surgery, my surgeon took a picture of the ball part of my left hip that he had taken out. It was not even a little bit like a round ball shape but was concave from the long-term rubbing of bone on bone after the cartilage had worn off.

My surgeon was shocked and told me I should have been in a wheelchair, not walking around as he had seen me doing. The pain I experienced in recovery was so much less than I had been living with every day for many years. It took a full year before I stopped tearing up as I explained that particular detail to people. Even if I had always been responsible for my angry thoughts, I was not responsible for how my hips formed while I was developing in my mother's womb.

Between the pain coming on so slowly and not being able to address my own needs, I didn't even notice it coming on until it was overwhelming. The pain had become so familiar that I just thought I needed to stop being such a wimp so I could be strong for my mom, my kids, and everyone else. It took a few months after the surgeries before I realized I was not lazy, rude or mean but had been in a major amount of pain. I am NOT saying that was an excuse for any bad behavior.

Still, my experiences didn't end there. I had been born with such odd-shaped hip joints that when I did begin to walk as a child, my muscles adapted to allow me to learn to walk, run, and climb just like a normal active child.

You see, of the three major muscle groups making up our buttocks, the Minimus, the Medius, and the Maximus, my body adapted by using only the Maximus and the Minimus muscles as I learned to walk. The Medius never developed.

Once my surgeries were over, my therapist couldn't understand why I wasn't moving my leg in the most simple exercise he could give me. My legs wouldn't budge no matter how much effort I put forth.

I was trying to walk with two overused muscles and one atrophied muscle. The working muscles had finally been put into the places where they were designed to be. My legs were used to interpreting my brain signals to move forward very differently. My old forward was now slightly sideways. Trying to rewire my brain, and reanimate that atrophied muscle at my age was interesting, to say the least. It's cute when a baby learns to toddle but it's just not as cute when a fifty-one-year-old does it.

I CAN Do Hard Things

My mother made public that I was wonderful. When we were alone, however, she would tell me that I wouldn't amount to anything. My hip surgeries were important recognition and further proof to me that I really could do hard things despite what I had been told. Before I went under the knife, I had been doing most family activities even through all the pain.

Only after recovering from my hip surgeries did I realize the gradually worsening pain I had been enduring. It had been such an incredible difference, but the pain had come on so slowly that I really hadn't perceived what was happening.

Through this experience, my identifiers, the ones that helped me see that I was not bad or wrong, clarified the limiting beliefs I had learned being raised by someone with NPD. I don't say this to blame her. It simply opened my eyes to understand that unrecognized influences, my pain, could affect my thinking, my emotions, and my life. I now look at many more aspects of a problem than only what is obvious so I can decide how to solve it with intention.

Deep Dive #4:

Our first caretaker is the biggest influence we have when we enter this world. If that influence is full of lies, manipulation, and gaslighting, we begin our lives with toxic confusion and grow to believe it is normal.

Getting back to those five plus influences I suggested you think about at the beginning of this chapter, and putting aside any judgments that show up, pick one influence that is negatively affecting your life right now. See if these questions help you work through your toxic confusion to make changes that could bring about a potential positive outcome. Again, it may help to write your answers for later contemplation.

Thinking about that one negative influence:

- **Can you recall where this influence began in your life?**
- **How is this one influence hurting your life? Could it be helping you somehow?**
- **What would your life look like without it?** Spare no details on this one. This one might be better to write out on paper so you can flush out everything you see within it. If it feels right, once you finish, you can shred it or burn it.
- **What is one thing you could do that would make this influence more of a benefit and less of a problem?**
- **What influences would you like to have in your life?**

When we look deeper, the thoughts associated with our long-experienced traumatic events create emotional trauma or CPTSD. Emotional pain is still pain. For some of us, the pain can become nefarious Demons and is debilitating. For others, it is a driving force that moves them to become something they would never have become without it. Either way, pain influences the way we act every day and when we notice it and choose to see it, we are better able to act with intention rather than absentmindedly react.

Any traumatic event can cause us distress, emotional breakdowns or outright nightmares. Our past will continue to influence us, knowingly or unknowingly. We are the only ones who can change our perception of our traumatic events that influence our lives from the time it happened to now. These events can motivate us to create something ultimately better or to create something worse.

I want you to be able to work through your own traumas one day. I have discovered that our original viewpoints can sometimes be simply us reacting to something from our own past, not something that needs to change for everyone else. In his book, *The Body Keeps the Score, Dr. Bessel Van Der Kolk* suggests that "autobiographical memories are not precise reflections of reality. They are stories we tell to convey our personal take on our experience."

I have discovered this myself as my thoughts about an event have changed over time with newer experiences and greater maturity.

We Are All Influencers

It can be odd to consider that we are all influencers, whether we realize it or not, for positive or negative. Some take a negative event and decide to make public changes to make the world a better place, being a positive influence as much as possible.

Others believe because of what was done to them, they are justified in harming others. These people are in so much emotional or physical pain from their life's traumatic events that they can't see clearly except to lash out and hurt others by causing the same pain they continuously feel.

We don't only influence others but ourselves as well. *(This is my favorite part!)*

You see, how we think about something influences how we react to it. When we change our perception about something, we change how the influence of it affects us, both the good and the bad. Our positive perception will often bring positive actions on our part and the opposite will also be true. When we perceive something as negative, we tend to act negatively in response to it.

There are so many books, podcasts and programs in the world right now that talk about affirmations or declarations because words are valuable to our minds. They are an incredibly powerful tool. It may not have been true, but being told enough times that I was a problem became a reality in my mind, one of my strongest Demons. This influential Demon became even stronger the more times I emotionally said out loud to myself how unworthy I was.

Our Demons' job is to keep us in our perceived truth. Intense feelings intensify what we perceive to be true. Any limit can become our truth if said enough times, especially if we add the emotional element. Our Demons are very good at their job.

But it also holds that our intrinsic truth can be rediscovered if said enough times outside of the narcissist's influence. We are the only ones living our lives, and when we honestly face what we feel while acknowledging our truth, we become our own best influencer. This most often goes beyond what we simply decide is true.

Human Freedoms

Attitude simply isn't enough to fix our circumstances. Trying, trying again, tweaking and trying yet again is sometimes the only way to move forward but it can often be debilitatingly discouraging.

It takes hope to get started but it also takes a lot of repeated, dedicated actions to make the larger more noticeable changes. This is where our attitude determines our outcome.

Just to be clear, agency is not doing whatever we want. It is not being free to act without regard to the consequences that are the result of our actions. Once we fully begin to understand the depth of what agency is at its core, we begin to see its amazing level of function in our lives. This clarity ties directly into, not only our responsibility to ourselves but also how we treat other people's agency. Including that *recognition in our actions is the balancing of our power.*

I was influenced by people who taught me that I couldn't learn to do things for myself so I instead, learned the opposite, that I have no power without permission from my authorities and everyone else is more of an authority than me. To a small degree, some giving up of our power is natural and appropriate, like when we are small children.

Agency Beats Influence

As we mature into awareness of who we are, we gradually realize that we have our own opinions, our own journey and that it can look vastly different from that of our parent's. This awareness is where our agency gives us the most power over our Demons. It is what helps us to create our lives the way we want despite what we are being told by them. It is mindfulness.

Understanding our agency is so vitally important; we can't ignore it and make mindful changes. If our Demons tell us we cannot embrace something, like sports, because our parents were not interested in them, we may give away our power to the Demons created because of our parent's choices and never discover that we actually enjoy sports.

If we believe we have no choice but to stay with a particular belief system because our parent taught us it was *the only way*, we lose the power to discover our own belief system. When we give away our power because of choices that our authorities have made, we give away our power to make our life our own.

This does not mean we can't follow our authorities' choices for us. It means we get to choose thoughtfully, mindfully, and with intention. We have the option to decide why we are doing a particular thing, and whether it fits with who we are personally or not.

We have the right to choose what we want in our lives, and even to let go of things that no longer work for us. We may have learned, as children, to keep our opinions to ourselves because it was not safe to go against our parental authorities. Even in the best of circumstances, we typically clash with our "perfect" or imperfect parent!

"The final forming of a person's character lies within their own hands."
— *Anne Frank*

Oh, what we can become...

The Choices We Make

I don't know where I first heard it but I was moved by a story about two adult males who were twins. There seem to be many versions of this story, but the one I heard goes something like this: one of the brothers was a career criminal and his twin was a CEO of an upstanding, successful company. Their father was addicted to alcohol and very abusive. Because they were twins, they had many of the same experiences but clearly had different perspectives.

As adults they were each asked the same question, "How did you get where you are?" They both gave the same answer. "If you had a father like mine, you would have turned out the same way." Their perceptions about their childhood and the decisions they made because of it were vastly different...clearly!

The brother who became the CEO knew who his father was, accepted his own flaws and created something successful for himself. He became balanced despite his upbringing. The brother who became a career criminal not only didn't accept who his father was, he thrust his lack of understanding onto others by thieving, harming or inappropriately controlling the lives of others because he wasn't in control of himself.

There are so many examples in history of people who had incredibly difficult experiences. Some chose to create positives only for particular people like Hitler, Mussolini and Mao Zedong. Some chose to find ways to benefit everyone, like Oprah Winfrey, Gandhi and Mandela. In the end, each of them made the choices that led to their influential lives. It is up to us to decide how our past runs us.

The truth is, our choices affect so many others whether we realize it or not. At first, I felt justified as a school bully until my actions were pointed out to me, and I chose to change my perception that my schoolmate deserved better than I had received at the hands of other's abusive actions.

As we grow in our authenticity, we continue to have diverse choices to make. We can pass on our traumas to others or let our particular pain created by someone else's behavior end with us. As long as we acknowledge our pain, we can see our troubled past as chains, and as a catalyst *for* change, breaking the link forever.

Truth Exists Outside of Our Understanding

Deep within our core, written upon our Intrinsic Blueprint, lives the truth of our best possible life. Our worth didn't disappear because no one else believed in us. Our superpower was never missing, it was simply invisible because we weren't allowed to recognize it. With that said, because it was trampled, we get to rediscover our worth for ourselves.

The things my Demons were telling me were based on lies and untruths. I overcame many of them through much difficulty and lots of effort to notice the few things I did right until I had more things I could feel I did right. I used my agency to build on each of those until I began to see that I actually had worth. This lesson was hard won, and took many years to first see, and more to believe.

My earlier inability to see worth in who I was didn't change the simple fact that I was the only one who could change my perception. My success in changing my circumstances was based heavily on my ability to see worth in myself. I had to learn to be okay with my failures, my disconnects, and my idiosyncrasies, no matter what my Demons said.

"Everything will be ok in the end. If it's not ok, it's not the end."
—*John Lennon*

Humble Confidence

Learning the truth of our worth is a process. Worth exists in all of us, and it is possible for us to believe it, to be humbly confident. This is a term I've come to love and attempt to emulate. It has served as a place for me to start so I can learn how to be unashamedly myself without being the problem my mother said I was for everyone. If others struggle with me, I can now take a step back—without taking it personally. I can also let others be where they choose to be without trying to change either one of us.

We must first recognize the thoughts that run through our own minds, otherwise we literally won't change a thing. As we keep working to notice those identifiers that show us what is hiding in the shadows, remembering what our responsibility is in the circumstances, we learn how to recognize and control our Demons. If we keep ignoring the identifiers that show up for us, our Demons will continue to wreak havoc. We don't have to go looking for them, just be willing to acknowledge them when they show up. By using our agency to first notice and then face what shows up, like when we are triggered, we can progressively gain back control over our lives.

Finding Balance

Balancing our lives takes practice and a willingness to notice what influences us. I now try to acknowledge both the negative and positive influences I receive as well as how I influence others.

As I acknowledge my perceptions on each of these, it can bring past traumatic memories to my present, and with great effort to not judge my past self through my current understanding, I am now better able to parse out how, and what I want to change.

Doing this consistently over the years, I have found that some of the things or people that I felt negatively about, I also felt positive feelings towards. It wasn't a simple case of getting rid of the negative and keeping the positive in my life. I needed to see both to balance my life.

Looking directly at my good and bad actions and recognizing the influences that led to why I did what I did, again giving myself grace, gave me possibilities to change from *reacting* to acting on purpose. I was now heading down a path of change that I had never even believed possible.

The memories I exposed from the corners of my mind were a part of what had fostered roles for me, behaviors for me to play...until I knew more. As I gained understanding about this beautiful dance of life, I had options. I could choose a better way of living for myself.

It was far into my adult years before I figured this out, but I was simply unable to change something for which I was unaware. Once learning this, my alternative was to continue to ignore reality, continue to create more of my own Demons, or persevere with the Demons I was given from my childhood and from others.

Acknowledging our past actions looks different for each of us. I know I say that often, but it is so true. We all look at our past actions differently. We also don't see things as adults the same as we did when we were younger, so acknowledging means we must take into consideration what our influences were at the time we took any of those past actions.

Our Incredibly Powerful Minds

I've read that there is science to show how our minds release corresponding chemicals with particular thoughts. This makes changing our mind something akin to going through a detox after being addicted to a serious drug. It can be extremely hard to do. We can't help but be influenced by all the things that have happened in our past, let alone all the people who have touched our lives for good or bad.

Yes, our lives are full of adversity, trauma and fears, which our Demons will use to control us. We can also recognize where our lives are full of adventures, excitement, and joy. Both have their part to play. As with our identifiers, if we bury our negative feelings when they show up, we will continue to give away power to run our lives.

When we begin to travel this particular path of acknowledging any of our emotions, those pesky Demons will begin to rise up in revolt. What we can do is begin to recognize how they are influencing us and decide which are no longer working for us. By looking directly at our Demons and continuing to notice our influences, we will gain confidence to use our agency—our internal, natural power—of which they are most afraid. Agency is their antithesis. Facing our Demons means we see them and acknowledge them. It is at that point that our agency becomes more of an influencer over our life than our Demons.

Simply looking at our Demons allows us the ability to see clearly enough to manage them, accept them or dismiss them on *our* terms. Long-term healing will require that we keep an open mind to how we are being influenced, by others and ourselves, so we can decide what to do with each as it shows up.

Realizing Your Boundaries

"A boundary is something you tell someone you will do, and it requires the other person to do nothing."

—Becky Kennedy

This chapter was, by far, the hardest one for me to write. It wasn't until recently that I really understood why it was so hard for me to set boundaries.

Our own boundaries are not something a narcissist can allow us to have because they would lose control over us. Like I mentioned when discussing unmet needs, narcissists cannot validate themselves. They believe that by controlling us, they will get validation, so they make us their source.

The problem with this is that validation only received through others is like trying to take a drink from a mesh sieve. It will never be enough. They will need more and more to satisfy their unquenchable thirst because validation from others is fleeting and quickly leaves a void that needs to be refilled.

The impact of being my mother's source of unrealistic validation meant that I followed my parent's example and didn't know how to validate myself which ultimately led to me not knowing how to trust myself. Because she would speak out of both sides of her mouth about my worth, I would often get emotional whiplash trying to figure out what she really felt about me. Was I the angel child or the monster she described?

That created a very difficult reality for me when it came to boundaries.

Boundaryless

In the summer of 1981, my family moved to Hobbs, New Mexico (NM). I was just entering my junior year of high school and, once again, did not exactly fit in. I felt like even more of an outsider than before with all these other students who had lived in this small town for generations.

I began looking for a community where I could belong. Since the one thing I felt good at was singing, I signed up for the high school's all girl choral choir named The Highlighters. We got a chance to perform in the Spring and the director asked us to memorize all five songs over the break.

Unfortunately, I never heard the part about us needing to have all five songs *completely* memorized by end of break and I lost my place in the choir. I felt like I had lost the only position I had in society. I no longer belonged to anything that was important to me personally.

Creating Chaos

I spent a lot of time during the rest of those two years of high school feeling lost and adrift. I became a kind of waif. I needed so much to be a part of something bigger than myself but, in pursuit of connection, my actions became detrimental. I slept around, I sought out parties to attend, I hung out with anyone willing to let me be a part of their group.

It seemed that my biggest attribute was that I didn't take recreational drugs. My friends would ask me to be the driver so they could get high. It seemed I only half fit in.

I felt so out of control during my senior year in high school but the only example I knew was how to attain that *craved-for* structure by seeking validation outside of myself. I needed something to radically change. In the last couple months of my Senior year, I signed up for New Mexico Military Institute (NMMI) in Roswell, NM during my high school's career fair. I had no experience with the military, but I knew that if I didn't do something drastic, my life would continue to spiral downward. I wanted more control over my own life.

Before I could take part in NMMI, I was to be first sent to attend Basic Camp, which is similar to basic training, with a bit more coddling for future officers—my definition.

I got my bus ticket and would be leaving for the eighteen-hour bus ride the day after my graduating class was having a huge party. I decided I needed one last binge before I spent the next six weeks not being able to drink. I found a friend who promised to take care of me so I could get completely smashed.

By the time the party was ending, my friend decided I was too drunk to bring home where her parents might discover what she had been doing, so she passed me over to the care of a mutual acquaintance. He did not take care of me, nor protect me. In fact, he indulged in his needs with my body by raping me.

The next morning, as I stepped onto the bus, I was filled with so many emotions that felt like they would explode out of me. Despite having a lifetime's experience of locking my emotions in a box so as not to upset my mother, it still took me the entire bus ride there to tamp them down into something barely manageable.

As well as a battery of medical tests, the first day mainly involved settling into our bunks with a couple of hours of drills. The next six weeks were filled with unfamiliar exercises, being yelled at in my face, and horrible food. To top that off, I felt sick the entire time. Unbeknownst to me, and despite having tested negative on day one of camp, I finished the entire six weeks pregnant.

After camp was over, NMMI was not able to give me a week to set things in order. I don't even remember if I told them I planned on getting an abortion but I was prohibited from attending if I couldn't start on that first day. I felt like this was my biggest failure yet, like I had graduated to complete and utter failure, if that was possible.

Boundaries Create Safety

Looking back on this, I have realized that, yes, I had needed healthy structure, but getting that structure from outside myself, going to a military college, would only have perpetuated me passing control from my mother to some other source outside myself.

What I hadn't yet figured out was, since I had to shove down all my feelings, thoughts and emotions about this event, this exacerbated the chaotic mess already within me. It would be my Personal Armageddon that would awaken my conscious mind to the particular necessity of internal structure and boundaries.

My mother's particular form of narcissistic characteristics was called vulnerable narcissism, so any rejection of her ideas for *my* life choices would often turn into her raging at me for being unsupportive of her parental authority. She encouraged me to believe that she was the only one who could help me create my life. In fact, narcissistic parents often encourage this belief, and we may grow up believing that we are somehow the ones who are bad or wrong. Because of the psychology of our parent, this untruth tends to stay unresolved while we are under their authority, and it makes having confidence in our worth later as an adult extremely complicated.

As children, our parents are seemingly omniscient; if they do something bad, we take on the meaning that we must be bad rather than believe our parents are bad.

Dr. Ronald Fairbairn, a Psychologist and Psychoanalyst, regarding children and child development, said, "It is better to be a sinner in a world ruled by God than to live in a world ruled by the Devil." This means, as a child, we took on the role of sinner, seeing ourselves as wrong because we needed to keep our narcissistic parent in the God role. It was too frightening to believe our parent was the devil. When this belief continues unresolved, we take that limiting belief into adulthood and never learn to trust ourselves.

Our particular narcissistic upbringing kept us from trusting ourselves, leaving us lacking the confidence to create safe boundaries as we were never allowed to before. Until we reach a point where we can learn to trust ourselves, we will continue to be enslaved to the limiting belief that setting boundaries is impossible. Our Demons will make sure of it.

To heal, however, setting boundaries is vitally important. They can lead to our emotional safety as well as our physical safety, though it is important to note that boundaries don't *guarantee* our safety. We can only control our own actions so we can only set boundaries to safeguard the places where we have control. By getting blindingly smashed, I gave away my power, and my safety became dependent on those to whom I gave my power. This action left any boundaries I might have had in the hands of others who clearly didn't have my safety in mind.

I will say that blame isn't the solution. The blame for me being raped doesn't lie with me nor the friend I asked to take care of me. Even if we each had our parts to play in this situation, no part of the situation meant I deserved to be raped under any circumstances.

We can't "just set them"

The typical formulas for most humans creating boundaries don't work for us: Decide what you want in life, create boundaries to keep on track, and *voila*! You arrive.

You and I must first get past the wrongness of what we were taught was our identity. Only then can we accept responsibility for the part we play in our lives, while still remembering to acknowledge the judgments that run through every aspect of our psyche. As we let go of what is not our responsibility, we will begin to recognize what is standing between us and our needed boundaries. We will see the influences standing in the way because we will begin to see how to deal with the influences blocking us.

My mother's view of my inability to concentrate, hold still or keep my mouth shut was incessantly berated as planned disobedience. According to her, I was purposefully acting out rather than being a normal kid. It wasn't until I was an older adult that I learned I had Attention Deficit Hyperactivity Disorder (ADHD).[11] As I came to realize that these characteristics were with me from childhood, I could finally see where her unwillingness to accept the many teachers who tried to suggest I get tested was her inability to accept anything different from what she wanted to believe about my perfect old soul status. Learning this helped me see first why I had certain tendencies, and second how to work with my uniqueness to balance my needs with finding a respectful balance for others involved with me.

There is a lot of learning we do later in life that was not afforded to us as children, and we have to feel safe before we are able to set boundaries. I find it rather ironic. We need boundaries to feel safe but we also need safety to set our boundaries. Safety is a huge problem for those of us who have grown up with a narcissistic parent.

---

11   ADHD – a neurodevelopmental disorder defined by impairing levels of inattention, disorganization, and/or hyperactivity-impulsivity. DSM V definition Section II pg 32

When I was a child, I felt emotionally unsafe to set boundaries because my mother would tear both me and my boundaries down if they didn't fit her version of "right". In high school, not knowing how to set boundaries turned into me being physically unsafe.

As we begin the learning process for how to set boundaries, our attempts may look like an impossible mess and we might wonder why we are even trying. Keep trying, looking at your circumstances, giving yourself grace for mistakes and being willing to learn not only what boundaries you need to set but how you need to set them for your unique situation. It will be completely worth it.

Deep Dive #5, part 1:

This boundaries chapter will have two parts in our Deep Dives. Let's first parse out some mental blocks…

1. Think of one location you are required to be but where you don't feel safe. **Write out as many things as you can think of that need to change so you could feel safe**. Don't hold back here, write it all!

2. Next, **tear up, shred or burn that page**. I burn mine because I feel like it's really gone and my personal thoughts are permanently private. It's a release of pent-up emotions.

3. Start again but this time **list a couple of ideas that are possible to change right now that will bring you toward feeling safer**. I am assuming that this one will be within the bounds of legal, no breaking laws here. It could be helpful to keep this page for later if you like.

4. **Go someplace where you feel safe and do something that fills you up**; gardening, playing music, drawing, sitting by the water, sitting in a forest, watching cars or people in a public place, etc. Maybe you try many of them until you find one that works for you.

5. While in this space reflect on the list you made of possible
    ideas that are doable right now. **Think of one or more neces-
    sary boundaries you will put in place to make your ideas a
    reality in your life. Spell out your boundary with as many
    details as possible.** These would include boundaries you have
    for how others interact with you, how you interact with others
    and especially how you might interact with yourself. This is
    another exercise that might be more useful writing out so you
    can reference your ideas later.

The longer we travel our healing journey, the more we will find the
confidence to validate ourselves. As we learn to self-validate, we will
become better able to receive healthy validation from others, giving us
more confidence to set our own boundaries.

I'm Okay

One of the first ways I learned to set boundaries was through changing my perceptions about myself. When I was in my late thirties, I met
a woman I initially judged harshly, but for whom I eventually learned
great admiration. With her hippy ways, I thought she was a bit of an
odd duck and I had no interest in many of the "*woo-woo*" things with
which she was involved. I did, however, feel something very down-to-
earth about her.

So, in spite of my original judgments, I decided to open up and began to actually listen to what she had to say. I discovered a link on her
colorful website that led me to finding another woman, Carol Tuttle,
whose teachings would begin my ability to self-validate.

Most every adult during my growing up years had not received, with
understanding nor acceptance, my fiery, passionate nature. I was mostly
tolerated, but certainly not encouraged to be me. Instead I was led to
believe I needed to be controlled. Through a book Tuttle wrote entitled,

It's Just My Nature, I learned for the first time, to love who I had been and who I was without feeling ashamed.

Tuttle describes four types of energy that we all embody. As whole beings, we contain them all but we tend to lead with one as a dominant. I identified as a type three: dynamic, energetic, determined, fiery and anything but calm. I was *not* what my mother thought of as a model child. Because of Tuttle's book, I now had a template for creating my boundaries that I didn't even know I needed. It was such a positive, pivotal time in my life. I learned that I wasn't actually broken, and neither was anyone else. I began to give myself permission to just be me.

My crescendo-like awakening came as I studied, observed and pondered. What I had been told as a child were my worst deficits – my loudness, my constant fidgeting, my quirkiness, I could now view as actual gifts, blessings, and talents to be utilized with care.

The best part...I was now learning how to *love* me for just being *me*. My passionate and fiery nature could be cherished even while I governed it. It often meant that I got things done. I could find the right place to be energetic because I didn't quit.

I learned to ask for my needs to be met at the right time and from the appropriate people. In other words, I could set boundaries for how I interacted with others. I could also set boundaries for how I let others interact with me because I was now gaining perspective on how my differences from others were valuable instead of seeing myself as *wrong*.

I still had such an amazingly long way to go, but I was finally moving in the direction of community *and* still being comfortable in my own skin. It was a game-changer! Since I was so much older when I finally learned this, I was still pretty awkward in my interactions.

I experienced added judgments from many of my Demons: "You should have figured this out long ago," "Why are you so weird?" and "No one is going to accept you so why even try?" Even though I had to navigate through all their lies, each time I accepted a new truth, it was such an amazing discovery in my journey.

Boundaries Are Personal

A true, healthy boundary does not create an attack on another person, it simply delineates where you end and they begin. A boundary also won't change how you feel about someone who has wronged you. A well-set boundary can, however, potentially keep them from harming you again. Remember, you can only set boundaries on your actions, not on the actions of others. As you are the only one who can decide your actions, others are the only ones who can decide their own actions. Your boundaries cannot change someone else's reactions to them but you can make requests.

Since we already know a narcissist would not care about your boundaries, and they might even see them as limits on their control, your setting boundaries needs to be done with intentional understanding to create that safety for yourself.

Dr. Becky Kennedy is a clinical psychologist who dedicates her time to helping parents understand healthy ways to parent children. In an interview she did with Dr. Andrew Huberman[12], she tells her definition of a boundary that I feel fits perfectly for those of us who are parenting ourselves because we didn't get that parental upbringing. Her definition of a boundary: A boundary is something you tell someone you will do, and it requires the other person to do nothing.

Because we are the only ones who can act for ourselves, learning to set our own boundaries helps *us* to create self-respect, something that was hard to come by during our growing-up years under the rule of our toxic parents. It is also true that we need a level of self-respect to even set our boundaries.

Until my Personal Armageddon, I hadn't any respect for myself and took full responsibility for all the bad things that ever happened in my life. Making changes for my daughter led me to the realization that I

---

12   How to Set Boundaries With Kids: Dr. Becky Kennedy & Dr. Andrew Huberman (YouTube – boundary definition @1:01-1:05)

needed to make changes within myself. This led me to the understanding that I needed to learn self-respect first if I wanted to be the example for her to have her own self-respect. I personally believe that children come to us innocent, which is why we must set healthy boundaries for them as they learn to set their own.

Learning self-respect as an adult, and holding to it, is a long process for those of us who grew up under the tyranny of narcissistic abuse but it is absolutely necessary. Anything that doesn't hold our self-respect is an identifier. It shows us where we need to notice something about our beliefs or actions. Balancing both learning our self-respect *and* recognizing our Demons' lies is a process. It is like creating a way to live in safe-vulnerability, where we are vulnerable but have created a safe environment to be so.

As we grow, we make personal boundaries with regards to how we choose to act and respond to other people. For instance, we keep certain information to ourselves. Even when speaking our minds, we can still hold some things back, out of respect for the company we are keeping or for our own safety if we are dealing with the narcissist in our lives. No matter what they say, we don't need to tell them everything. They are not living our lives, we are.

One of my current personal boundaries is to avoid people that focus on the negative. For instance, I'm fine with a bit of griping, because sometimes it creates conversation that incites change. However, people who set up their address living in the negative are people with whom I choose not to interact for very long. I do, unfortunately, remember being there myself.

When we are unsure of our boundaries or if we don't have them in place to best fit *us*, we will find our lives are littered with unsolvable problems. Our boundaries give us a base from which to work. It's a place to start as we interact with the world. Knowing our own boundaries sets the stage for us to discern where our Demons are trying to retake control. That information is useful in creating clearer paths while still making the changes we personally want. Deciding on your own boundaries is partially cultural, partially personal and can be attuned to how we were or were not nurtured.

Successfully figuring out what our boundaries are will look more like a beautiful dance we do with others that has imperfect, though flowing moves. When we learn to set meaningful and mutually respectful boundaries, this dance flows back and forth as we twirl around in beautiful, choreographed synchronicity.

My Boundaries

By the time my mother was diagnosed, I was fifty-four. I had become comfortable *enough* in my own skin to take on stronger boundaries with her, especially as the enormity of her disorder became clear to me.

For the first year after learning that my mother had NPD, I floundered my way through every stage of grief multiple times. Once I wrapped my head around what boundaries I needed to set, I again tried to reconnect with my difficult mother.

Unfortunately, I didn't yet realize the very definition of her psychological disorder made a deeper connection with her an impossibility. I hadn't fully comprehended how alone I had felt throughout my life. My entire childhood was full of attempts to have a deeper connection with my mother, and I was once again traumatized as I finally came to the realization that I would never be able to have a healthy, parent-child connection with her. I often found myself feeling like an exploding volcano, oozing pain over all my family and friends, and no one understood what I was going through, including me. I had to create safe zones not only *for* myself but with myself.

Boundary One:

My first boundary was with myself. Because NPD is misunderstood by the general public, as I grew in my boundary-setting with my mother,

I came to realize that most people didn't believe she couldn't actually love me, that to her I was just an extension of herself rather than my own individual. In public, they saw a "perfect" parent. That left me to set a boundary for how not to engage with other people's misconceptions about the love my mother was or was not capable of offering.

Boundary Two:

My next boundary was with my mother regarding how I spoke with her. If she called me unexpectedly, I may or may not pick up the phone. If I did pick up and she started telling me, "You should call me more often," or "You don't call me enough," I would simply tell her I needed to get off the phone or had something I needed to get back to. Explaining to her why never went well so I learned to keep my explanations to myself, knowing I was doing what was right for my own mental health.

There were many times I didn't call her back because I couldn't get past the messages she left, "Hello, this is mom, remember me?" or "This is your mother who you should call more." It was particularly annoying when I had just spoken with her less than twenty-four hours prior. She told me she wanted me to call her daily. I wasn't going to do that. It helped that I lived a few thousand miles away, so calling was the only way she could interact with me, and that gave me greater ability to set the necessary boundaries for my well-being as I learned them. This reestablishing of communication terms, I realized, was a necessary boundary for me and my mental health.

Boundary Three:

Another boundary I set while clearing out the traumas in my Shadow–side was to allow myself, as a mother, to "have a time-out." I hung a small pillow on the door to my bedroom on which I had stitched, "DO NOT DISTURB!" I used this when I felt especially anxious around my kids. Timeout for me might have been only as long as I needed to keep from raising my voice.

Because my mother got physically abusive when she felt unable to control me, I learned, by her example, that abuse would be that next step. I wanted nothing to do with it, but because it was so ingrained in my history, I needed boundaries to process my stress.

Before my understanding of the importance of boundary setting, I was a twenty-four year old mother of two kids aged five and one. Once, my oldest daughter did something that made me so mad I actually envisioned myself throwing her out the window. This scared me so much that I turned on the television, sat my two kids in front of it and, after locking the door, I took a walk around the block to cool off. All the way around the small block of my married student housing, I thought to myself, "If they take them away from me, at least it won't be because I beat them." I wanted to end that family trend forever.

I hadn't realized I was setting a boundary with myself to protect my kids but that was exactly what I was doing.

Boundaries Are Flexible

When we take stock of our simplest identifiers, we begin to see our Intrinsic Blueprint's light peek through.

I had heard people say that mothers are the cornerstone of a happy home. Remember when I talked about believing that nobody can be happy if mom isn't happy? My mother twisted this truth until it became something nefarious. What was being said about the importance of mothers in the home had nothing to do with being responsible for her happiness.

While I was raising my own kids, and because I didn't have a better example, the idea that my kids had to be responsible for my happiness turned into me expecting them to do what they were told, for their happiness, of course. Learning about agency was the identifier that helped me see how my Intrinsic Blueprint, my internal truths, were against any other person being responsible for my happiness.

We can use our Intrinsic Blueprint to know where our personal boundaries need to be set. It may or may not be obvious what those boundaries need to be but a crucial point here is that these boundaries will change as we change. If we let them, they will often grow with us and we will learn to find safety in our boundaries as we begin to build on our Intrinsic Blueprint.

Other benefits of setting boundaries will present themselves as we grow to understand that what we have learned through our painful experiences has now become information we can utilize to set even better boundaries for even more safety. It's information to better our lives instead of devastating, end-of-the-world traumas that continue to demolish anything we create.

I'm speaking of my own original viewpoints here. At one point in my life, every negative event was a devastating, life-ending threat. I didn't understand why no one else was as upset as I was at whatever I was going through at that moment. Learning to hold to my boundaries created a vantage point from which I could see my Demons more clearly, and I became more capable of rooting out the dramas in my life.

Life started to become something worth living and exciting to experience instead of something to fear. Rather than win or lose, I could finally choose to win and learn, more of the time.

Boundaries give us this permission to feel what we feel and experience life our way while not hurting others simply because we are in pain. They are meant to protect our lives to be what is best for us and they are meant to change *our* lives, not the lives of others. We can only be responsible for how we feel. We are not responsible for how others feel.

Deep Dives #5.5, part 2:

As we heal, our mind opens up to things we didn't realize were possible. It expands and sees new avenues we hadn't seen before while we learn to recognize the things in our past that are no longer working for us.

For this second part of the exercise, I want you to recall the boundaries you thought of that were doable right now. Remember, a boundary is something we tell others we will do but requires the other person to do nothing.

1. **What is your part in making this boundary work for you?**
2. **Work out some ideas you can do if your boundary is crossed.**

   » **Bonus questions:** Only answer these if you feel safe with the questions you've already been answering. If you don't, give yourself permission to skip these. **What is the worst that would happen if you never went back to that place where you feel required to be? What is the best that would happen if you never went back to that place where you feel required to be?**

3. **Decide when would be a good time to act on this new boundary you have thought of.** Set a date to start acting on this new boundary.
4. Before you start your new boundary, find a safe person in whom you fully trust to help you stay accountable to yourself. Work out with this person the details for how they can best support you. Let them know the date you plan on implementing your boundary.
5. **Implement your boundary.** Sometimes it can be as simple as telling others your boundary. Sometimes it will be more complicated. Be aware that when you make changes, unsafe people will push back on your boundary. They don't like change they don't understand. Narcissists don't like changes they haven't implemented. Holding to your necessary boundary is you showing integrity for yourself, something your narcissistic caretaker couldn't allow you to do. It will feel very unfamiliar, hence your support person.

Forgiveness

A friend once told me that narcissists can't help what they do, so we should forgive them for their abuse. She said that once I forgave my mother, I would be free from all the pain that she caused. I don't personally believe that is how forgiveness works.

Forgiveness is widely believed to be the end goal of all healing, but because we are each so unique, it doesn't look the same for everyone. Besides being a uniquely personal journey, forgiveness has many levels we will reach while on that journey. Let me start with what I think forgiveness is not!

What forgiveness isn't:

- **Forgiveness doesn't automatically happen if we decide to ignore the person who hurt us.** Associating with my mother as little as possible did not mean I was not forgiving her. It meant I was finding my autonomy, something she would attempt to sabotage whenever we interacted.

- **Forgiveness does not need someone to suffer because they harmed you.** I didn't need my mother to suffer for all the abuse she put me through. I just had to learn that my life had to be separate from hers for me to be truly safe. This was only able to happen once I became an adult.

- **Forgiveness is not forgetting what happened.** There was so much known and unknown abuse for me. Forgetting it all, no matter how hard I tried, was not a reality. What was possible was releasing each Demon she filled my psyche with once I found them and replacing them with my own healthier alternatives to thinking.

- **Forgiveness is not excusing what was done.** My mother abused me physically, verbally and emotionally. These acts were done by her choice. Her disorder does not excuse her responsibility for these actions.

- **Forgiveness is not about how I feel about her.** I have had many varied emotions towards my mother, some positive and many negative. Underneath I always loved the idea of my mother but I never felt I liked her. Her diagnoses made clear to me why, even though I still loved her as a mother. Getting to this point on my journey did, for me, mean I had to allow myself to hate her for a time.

- **Forgiveness is not about reconnecting.** I never chose to sever my ties with my parental narcissist, though I know people who have. Through my research, I learned that she would never be able to have a healthy mother-and-daughter relationship with me. Once learning this, I chose not to continue that fruitless endeavor.

When we take into account the concept that as children, we were unaware our toxic parent had a psychological disorder, we choose what to do with that information. Whether they were purposefully harming us or were compelled by their disorder was outside of our understanding. It may have been all we knew so what was actually abuse was often our "normal".

Even though we didn't understand our treatment was abusive, once we became adults, we were still left foundationally destitute of the healthy love and true acceptance we needed as children to actually grow into healthy adults. They did what they did, and we grew up in a whirlwind of constant trauma created by them. They still made our childhood a living hell, whatever their reasons. We, in turn, have agency to either pass on that example to others or to choose not only a better way for us to live but also to make the lives around us better too, as Mandela and Oprah did.

What It Looks Like For Me

Forgiveness for me looked like learning to live my life how I believe a healthy mother would have wanted, one who didn't have NPD. After all, this was how I wanted my children to live their lives. It looked like me knowing that I was acknowledging my mother for her efforts no matter what she said about my actions. Forgiveness for me meant I learned to laugh—a real, honest heartfelt laugh that came from the pit of my stomach. It meant not always sharing with her when something went right in my life because what was right for me was most often different from her ideals. It meant living my life in a way that I could wake up each morning excited for the new day, being grateful for all the experiences that came into my life or that I created.

Nothing would change on her end. Forgiving was an acknowledgment of where I needed to set my own personal boundaries with her. This way I was able to create a safe space for myself and let go of how I felt about her continued manipulations to *fix* my life. Others may choose differently, and that is the beauty of agency. Our agency is ours to control.

Discovering Our Boundaries

When we hold to our boundaries, other people will change in their response to them. That's true in healthy and unhealthy relationships. When a healthy boundary works, creating a wonderful ebb and flow, it reinforces both parties' safety. The more healthy the boundary, the more mutually beneficial and comfortable each willing party is with it.

Because boundaries look so different for each of us, we will each find different ways to discover and keep them. I prefer to journal about my thoughts because I like writing. From the book, "The Artist's Way," by Julia Cameron, I learned to do morning pages. Morning pages are three pages of stream of conscious writing when you first get up in the morning. I like that you don't have to worry about grammar, punctuation, spelling, or language. You write anything that comes to your mind, and you don't reread it nor do you let anyone else read it. It serves to get out of your head all those thoughts that block your creative self. I think Julia says it all in this quote, "The morning pages will change you!"

Not a Writer?

A client of mine who has been determined to get the better of her Demons absolutely *hates* writing. She would go to great lengths to avoid it. Until we both realized what was happening, we could not figure out why she was not getting the results she so desperately wanted.

Once her absolute hatred of writing became clear to both of us, she chose instead to use her cell phone's voice recorder. She has since found great success in recording her thoughts whenever they pop up. She can even do it in the car while she is doing errands. She told me once that she hasn't yet figured out how to do it in the shower but I have no doubt she will find a way. She is extremely resourceful.

Note: If you feel unsafe about writing how you feel, burn the pages when you are done but still write to get them out of you.

As I journal, I notice patterns that emerge. Sometimes I just complain in my journaling but maybe my complaining turns into journaling about what I can do to *fix* whatever I'm complaining about. I often take those ideas and create a list (more writing) of what I want to change, what I need to do to make that change and even how it might look once the changes are made. Next I will put the first steps onto my to-do list for the current day. The next day I may add the next steps, if appropriate, until ultimately that change is made or the process toward that change has become a habit. I have done all these steps in comparative levels of completion.

When I follow through, I often discover the lies my Demons are telling me so clearly that those particular lies no longer have power over my day-to-day life. It gives me permission to feel what I feel, as I notice my past traumas in my Shadow-side, and helps me balance them with my Light-side.

When to set boundaries will be determined by your desire to choose your life's direction. The desire to be in charge, instead of being out of balance because your Demons run your life, will help you learn which boundaries to set that work for you. Over time you can adjust them to fit the changes you are making.

Bottom line, the time is now. Now, tomorrow, the next day *and* the next. Setting boundaries is not a one-and-done exercise. It is a lifelong practice…but only if you want to be the one in charge of your life.

To do this, let's first look at how NOT to set boundaries.

How Not to Set Boundaries

Insist others change: Boundaries are personal. We can only change ourselves. If someone is doing something unacceptable to us we can only decide where *our* line in the sand is, not theirs.

Creating hooks for someone: Deliberately asking for an extremely difficult boundary for someone else helps no one, not even yourself.

Setting boundaries for others to hold for us: As Dr. Kennedy suggests, boundaries need to be what you can do, not what someone else should or should not do.

Now that we have some ideas how NOT to set boundaries, let's look at some things to consider when we do set them for ourselves.

Create boundaries for ourselves that we can make and manage: Again, boundaries are personal. Boundaries often require that we make changes. The changes we make for ourselves are more personal than the ones others make for us. They also have a tendency to last longer.

Be willing to update boundaries as we learn: Our boundaries will be continuously changing as we grow. When we've grown beyond the need for a particular boundary, we can set a new one that works for us in that moment. We can either let go of that outgrown boundary or update it to fit our new circumstances.

Create boundaries with ourselves to overcome failures: Most of us are harder on ourselves than we are on others. This especially holds true for people who have been abused. For example, my boundary for deciding to only talk with my mother when I felt emotionally safe to do so became my decision. I didn't ask her to never call. Occasionally, I just didn't answer.

Having boundaries with others is important, but keeping boundaries with yourself allows those boundaries with others to work. It creates the self-respect one needs to function with others as well as oneself. It is one of the most important things you will do in your healing process.

The Process
of Healing

"Life Can Be Beautifully Difficult!"

—Lisa Sitze

I n this chapter, I want to talk about tools you already have, or can develop, that will help you create that unique life you are now able to look forward to designing.

Healing Emotions

There are so many avenues to travel if one is looking to understand our emotions. This section contains just one road I took but it changed my life.

What do you think of when someone says the phrase, emotional intelligence?[13] The term was coined by Peter Salovey and John D. Mayer in an article they published in March of 1990 for a psychology journal entitled, "Emotional Intelligence," which has since come to be known

---

13   Emotional Intelligence – a type of intelligence that involves the ability to process emotional information, and use it in reasoning and other cognitive activities. APA.org Dictionary; emotional intelligence

as EI. I am paraphrasing here how, in the article, they theorize that EI comprises a set of four particular skills: perceiving and identifying emotions, using emotions to make thought possible, understanding emotions, and managing emotions.

I felt that, if these were indeed skills, then I either had them or I could learn them. This was not something I recognized when I was learning how to do this but through writing this book, I can see now the path my healing journey took.

The simple version, first I had to learn to recognize my emotions. This was the only part I felt was possible for me at a basic level. I hadn't yet figured out how to identify my emotions with words, so I needed to learn this. Putting what I felt like were arbitrary words to my feelings was a long and arduous journey but it was how I learned to do the second part, using my emotions to think. How I felt would often turn into what I thought about my emotions. I learned to think about my emotions as mine regardless of what others said about how I was supposed to feel.

What I thought about my emotions led me to more understanding of what my emotions were, why my emotions were there, and set me up for the fourth part of learning how to manage or regulate my emotions. Through this, I eventually learned to allow myself to have whatever emotions were there while still keeping them from spilling over onto others.

My ADHD made regulating particularly difficult but my need to make life better for my daughter was a great motivator. My consistent determination led to being able to work toward, and eventually work through this each time I needed to figure out how I was feeling about a traumatic event. Each time I did this, the planning and achieving part proved to be fairly easy once I was able to express and consciously, albeit authentically, regulate my emotions.

My agency gave me the ability to do all of these things once I was no longer being drawn back into what my mother deemed right for me. I could finally determine, for myself, what was right for me. After her death, I became even more free to pursue my own direction for my life.

The more I learned about what I actually felt, and the more I allowed myself to have my feelings, the closer to my ideal life I was able to live.

Bottom line, feeling our feelings is a must. When they are allowed to exist, and when we learn to regulate them, i.e. express them in healthy ways, they become direct pathways to our Intrinsic Blueprint that provide information for how to achieve our personal authenticity.

Taking time to acknowledge and feel what we feel frees us to use our agency to manage or let go of emotions that no longer work for us. Sometimes I need to sit with my negative emotions rather than try to replace them with preferred ones. This basic act is us showing ourselves a level of self-respect that empowers us to not only recognize our authenticity but to utilize it with confidence. This was made crystal clear to me when I learned of my mother's diagnosis.

Clarifying Diagnosis

For me, this was the biggest breakthrough of my entire healing journey. It took a full year for me to do enough research to fully recognize the depth of the effects that her NPD had on my childhood. Even after I realized the loss of affection and all the unfulfilled needs every child requires, it was yet another year of me going through all the stages of grief that ended in anger. That was when my healing journey led to the need for me to allow myself permission to hate her.

For me it was her death that granted me the freedom to fully live the healing I had been attempting over so many years prior. I hope you can learn to live your life your way before the narcissist in your life dies. I know it is possible because I have witnessed it in the lives of others.

I intensely dislike the adage, "If I can do it, you can do it," so I won't say that to you here. I've bought into that so many times and the needed variables that fell into place to make it possible for another person to do "whatever it was" so easily have looked different for me. It seemed motivational, until I repeatedly failed and ended up feeling like a complete loser, again. "If I can't even do that *simple* thing, maybe I really am hopeless like my mother told me so many times." Wow, did my Demons nurse *that* thinking along! Instead I will say, what I do know is, when you utilize your agency, you will find healing in your own way, because, though we all have this superpower, you use yours in a way that comes from your unique Intrinsic Blueprint.

"It's never too late to be who you might have been."
– George Elliot

What This Means For Us

Our emotions being more connected to executive power than our logic does not mean we cannot learn to make rational decisions. It means that when we are not attentive to them, too often our emotions will influence our decisions outside of rational thought. Not recognizing our emotions, they will eventually take over our actions, spewing out onto everyone and everything around us like an exploding volcano.

When we do take on the work of understanding the way we see our emotions, we actually change the way they affect us. We become more conscious when we allow ourselves to have our emotions. We have the right to feel what we feel. They are a part of our Light-side and who we are as a whole person.

Balancing these two means acknowledging our feelings, which tells our conscious mind that we matter, our feelings matter, the way we view our experiences matter, and there will be an identifier to each and every emotion we are feeling.

As children to a narcissist, we were not allowed to experience our emotions if they were uncomfortable for our parent. Not being allowed to process through our emotions meant we never learned to emotionally regulate. It is a delicate but crucial balance we need for a healthy adulthood.

Deep Dive #6:

Balancing takes practice…note: Because this exercise can be emotionally difficult, I suggest you do this one with support from someone you trust.

Pick a medium i.e., writing, painting, gardening, dancing, exercising, singing, sewing, sculpting, hiking, painting, drawing, or whatever is your favorite means of creativity, and allow your mind to recognize your emotions. I tend to use writing because I use multiple senses. I see the words on paper, feel the pen in my hand and read them aloud to myself as I think about my next sentence.

Next, pick one emotion that showed up and decide how you feel about feeling it. Yeah, I know that sounds strange but recognizing and acknowledging our emotions means we give ourselves permission to feel them so we can be mindful of them. Instead of pushing them away because society says we shouldn't feel anger, sadness or some other emotion we clearly feel, we can learn to sit with it so we know what we want to do with it. Until we sit with it, we are just feeling it, not experiencing it.

Use your chosen medium to acknowledge, not justify, but acknowledge, that we have the right to feel that emotion. When we justify an emotion, we try to show or prove why we should feel that way. When we acknowledge it, we accept how we are actually feeling, and we gain control over making decisions for our life rather than that emotion running things.

Ponder it, feel it and decide where it needs to be to best serve you. Not only do you have the right to feel what you feel, you also have the right to hold on to negative emotions if you decide that works for you. Though I don't feel we have the right to harm others, we can choose to hate our parent for a time if that allows us the ability to find our balance. We may eventually choose to let that emotion go.

Motivations and Shifting

In a paper written by Maslow entitled: "A Theory of Human Motivation," he describes motivations as based on our needs. If we are motivated to upgrade our thinking we will find a way to reach that next level. I was motivated to change my thinking because I saw how my current actions were creating for my daughter an inability to live as a child outside of adult concerns.

We may act due to external motivations, for example, physical beatings if we don't do the dishes the specific way our parent requires us to. Our healing journey is dependent on what internally motivates us to take that next healing step. If we are unmotivated to make the necessary changes (i.e., stop eating cheese), we may find ourselves complaining about the reactions our body is having rather than accepting what is causing that reaction even after it is obvious. Sometimes we get disastrous results before making particular changes. I am now dairy-free.

Motivations shift over time. By looking at our current life, noticing where we want things to be different can help us decide how much effort we are motivated to make to create actual changes. There will also be times when we don't make changes at all.

Trust *your* process.

To work for you, your motivations need to be based on your Intrinsic Blueprint. Because they are so personal, the group of motivations that work for me may not work for you. It depends on your personal needs and current preferences.

In his book, *Wanting,* Luke Bergis suggests we are always wanting, and are always motivated to do something, eat, sleep, play, or interact with others. It's human nature to need, to want, and to progress. When we don't progress, we eventually die. A healing journey is a progression we as abuse survivors cannot forgo.

Processing Your Healing

When we are emerging out of a life of abuse, we are learning something completely new. Because it is unfamiliar to us, we need to take baby steps until we get comfortable enough to take bigger strides.

One thing my attic dream taught me was the value of working on one part at a time, no matter how big the mess. I wasn't too much, too difficult or a problem to be fixed or solved. It was especially not required that I be beaten on a regular basis so I would comply with my mother's demands. I had valuable insight, and it was her specific job to support me in realizing this as I grew.

The way I choose to utilize my agency now is specific to my circumstances. Sometimes I fix something I see as a problem. Sometimes I ignore it and accept the consequences. Neither is right or wrong. Though I try to pay attention to how my actions will affect other people, the way I now choose to use my superpower is to work from my Intrinsic Blueprint one identifier at a time.

In her book, *But It's Your Family,* Dr. Sherrie Campbell talks about cutting ties with her toxic family and how complicated and difficult that was to do. Not only was she leaving the only family she ever knew, she was met on all sides by people who had no idea the abuse she endured. It is incomprehensible to most people that a mother would be incapable of loving or sacrificing for her child's needs. It's even more absurd, to more normal families, that a mother would secretly view her own child as a threat rather than a person needing her nurturing care.

My mother was only loving to me when others were watching or when I was doing what she wanted. In her view, her responsibility to raise me was as a demonstration for others to see her parenting capabilities. To encourage me to be responsible for how the world viewed her parenting, my mother would often ask, "What will others think about me if you do that?"

When we are conscious about what our Demons are and where they come from, it frees us to choose how we will work with them and gives us more power to thoughtfully decide the consequences and by default our outcomes. We can make the more profound changes in our lives that we have been needing for so very long.

It was difficult for me to trust my process since it seemed to be all over the place at a time when my mind needed direction. My journey was not linear by any sense of the word. I don't think anyone's healing can be.

Too often I forgot what I had learned and relearned those ideas while I was in the process of learning something completely different. Sometimes I did this so many times for the same concept that it made my head spin.

Writing this book has made this so poignant to me. I had this idea to sit down and write how I went from point A to point B, and continued down the alphabet as I learned concepts from being codependent to independent in a linear fashion, making my journey understandable to others. Not a thing. I still find some things I thought I worked through show up again and again. For instance, I catch myself blaming my online game character for not gliding or attacking or flipping the way my head thought they should. Luckily, I can often notice and adjust my thinking.

If we can embrace this, we will ironically move faster on our healing path because we are no longer getting in our own way. It can be terrifying but eventually those uncomfortable identifiers can motivate us to make those changes we had been trying hard not to see, like when I finally got my hips replaced after years of ignoring the signs.

It might take a while to recognize those habitual responses that the narcissist trained into us but as we continue to try, it will become more and more our own life rather than their dictated way for us to be. We *never* get too old to change.

Acting Vs Coasting

As I've mentioned before, comfort and familiarity have common ground. Our Demons are more comfortable in the familiar but something that is familiar isn't always good for us. We are familiar with the abuse we were raised with like the verbal or physical. Unfortunately, we may have passed some version of them down to our children as normal.

Comfort as well can sometimes be a trap. As children, changes may not have been possible no matter how uncomfortable we were, so we learned how to find a level of solace within our discomfort. If we choose now to act as adults, we can revisit this and learn how to acknowledge where we currently feel obligated to coast in the familiar masking we had to maintain for our parent.

It's not only our Demons that find familiarity more comfortable, we humans prefer it as well. Stepping out of our familiar comfort zones is difficult. As we step away from abuse, the world can be ridiculously, intensely scary, even if freedom from abuse is something we truly want. Before we start, we need to remember to give ourselves grace when we are changing our lives, especially our old, but familiar ways of thinking. This is where needs come into play for me.

To continue *my* healing journey, I have to keep acknowledging that I *need* to recognize all the familiar Demons that are running my life. With my ADHD, it can be difficult to do this because my neurodivergent brain doesn't work the same as someone with executive functioning intact. I can't simply decide to make something happen. Instead I've learned that both external and internal motivation needs play a big part for me to take action. Learning this about the way my brain works made it more possible for me to give myself grace when I didn't function the way the world believed I should, and I've been able to continue working through my traumas, sometimes one at a time.

Passing the Problem

I wish I could say that my efforts to allow my daughter to make her own mistakes gave me the ability to create the perfect environment for all my kids. I didn't really know how to give my children space to learn their way, and I rarely allowed them time to process through their emotions. Modeling the parenting style I grew up with, I thought I was saving them from confusion by telling them what they should be feeling at a given moment. I thought I knew what they should be feeling. I did eventually learn how to give them time to process, but not until all my children had grown up and moved out.

Successful personal growth allows for consequences to be acknowledged and reckoned with, regardless of whether one sees them as good or bad. This way they become identifiers to use as information, not detriments to shut one down. If I had acknowledged how my children really felt, they could have learned the ability to work through their emotions rather than their emotions running them. It's called "emotion regulation," and that is something Dr. Becky Kennedy talks about. It was my children's job to feel their emotions and to learn. My job was to set boundaries and help them process their emotions.

Luckily my children learned this idea and are now letting my grandchildren process their emotions while still setting appropriate boundaries. It is beautiful to watch!

Progressive Healing

I've made a few leaps and bounds over the years but I have mainly changed my life one small step at a time. I didn't have an overall plan. My original motivation was to take control of my life when I graduated from high school so I didn't continue to spiral out of control. Unfortunately, I was unaware that what I really needed was internal structure. Because I was searching for external structure, though I did slow my downward spiral, my changes were minimal.

Because I was unable to create internal structure for myself at that time, my childhood training to be codependent led me to my Personal Armageddon where I became externally motivated to find a way to allow my daughter the freedom to make her own choices. I still didn't know what I was doing but this is where my obligation to help others showed up as a benefit for me as well as my daughter. I was scared but I couldn't give up on *her*. With a lack of understanding of my own worth, I was only minimally motivated to make changes for myself but I felt my daughter was worth me changing myself, and I was determined to keep trying to be that example no matter how many times I felt I failed.

> *"The mask of self importance hides loneliness,*
> *lack of confidence and lack of worth."*
> — *Cleveland Clinic*

Healing From the Masks

Because our history with narcissistic abuse likely taught us to hide our truthful feelings, it often felt unsafe to be honest about them, even with ourselves. We may have created beliefs to be less noticed by our abuser, developing a mask to show the world what the narcissist trained us to be so they could look like a good parent. With our new understanding, we now have the ability to change that by setting our own boundaries to discover *our* authentic selves as we step outside the toxic boundaries that were created for us.

Let's look a bit closer at how David Hawkins' energy theory research works here. According to Hawkins, emotions start as sensations within our body, and our thoughts interpret them as feelings. When we learn to acknowledge and potentially change our thoughts, we can be more in control of our feelings. Ultimately we have the power to create boundaries that work to emanate our authentic self. It is possible to be confident yet humble, authoritative without being a dictator, giving and serving without compromising our standards, and being contrary when we need to hold to our truth while still maintaining civility. All these things are possible.

Healing from narcissistic abuse is a very personal journey, but also one that cannot be done without involving others. Unfortunately, our experience with our narcissistic parent created so many convoluted personal traumas, it makes bringing others into our healing journey very uncomfortable.

Simultaneous Healing

As I began to heal, I began to see others through a different lens. The things that were previously annoying or irritating to me, I started to see them as what made that person who they are as they were living their own life. Maybe their experiences included me. Or, I might choose not to be included in their chosen life experiences.

Our life choices really are up to us.

Humans are designed to be social creatures, some more than others but we all need interaction with other people. There are two sides to interacting with others. One side is that we have a part to play, which gives us the power to act for ourselves, our agency. The other is that we are not the only ones playing a part. The very definition of interacting with someone else is that another person is involved. They play a part as well, for good or bad.

Because as children of narcissistic abuse we are constantly working to find a place of safety, how we let others show up in our lives is vitally important. When we come far enough to feel we are safe, we are better able to take back our power without throwing others under the proverbial bus. Before we get there, however, we might need to learn how to allow others to be offended while giving ourselves grace to feel hurt or rejected. We are still learning to find our safe space. This is crucial. When we get to the point where we are working with others to help us through our traumas, we must feel a sense of safety.

It's Not All in Our Mind

Sometimes we will mentally work through our issues but our body has not had time to process them. We need to let our body catch up with our new perspectives just as much as we need to give our mind time to process them. Dr. Peter Levine developed the concept of Somatic Experiencing. It is a recognition of how the body naturally holds onto but cannot always heal our traumas.

Because our mind experiences things different from our body, we need to recognize how our body internalizes our traumas. We can know what to do, have all the learned answers and still get triggered when someone makes a particular comment, looks at us in a particular way, or touches us in a way that brings back a traumatic childhood memory. When we allow our body time to catch up to our mind's new understanding, balancing becomes progressively possible.

Remember that I mentioned the book, *The Body Keeps The Score*? Well, in it, Dr. Van Der Kolk "uses scientific advances to show how trauma literally reshapes both body and brain, compromising sufferers' capacities for pleasure, engagement, self-control, and trust."

We can only process through traumas to the best of our mind's *and* our body's ability.

Healing Our Relationship with the Narcissist

It is work to work through our traumas. We do tend to naturally avoid our Shadow-side. If we find a trauma that we want to work through but find we really aren't ready yet, looking at it, acknowledging it and putting it back for later can become a very real possibility.

As I discussed in the boundaries chapter, through my journey to forgiveness with my mother, there was another step. I had to *allow* myself to "hate" my mother so I could acknowledge my feelings before they would stop infecting me from the inside. Denying my hatred wasn't making it go away. On the contrary, those feelings were consistently dragging me down, undermining my attempts to heal and generally being an infectious mess behind the mask I presented to the world. I have personal experience why we don't want to take off our masks.

I didn't choose to keep hating her. I honestly didn't want to. It was not part of my Intrinsic Blueprint or my personality. I did, however, have to acknowledge my feelings to release their hold on me. It took me over a year to begin releasing them. I had to face my Demons before my life with my mother, and her actions towards me no longer had control over me. That was the only way I could see what was my responsibility and what was hers, whether she accepted her part in our relationship or not.

I put many traumas back into my Shadow-side multiple times before working through them fully. I still have negative feelings about how she raised me, but they are no longer attached to unrealized emotions. I still feel them, but since they're now visible, *they no longer run me.*

The same can be true for you.

Our unrealized traumas won't go away until we do face them. They will wait for us. The more intense ones are a bit more difficult to release. I would suggest getting professional help with these. Being physically or emotionally uncomfortable is our body's way of telling us something is out of harmony in our lives and needs to be looked at on a deeper level. It's required to do so if we want to be emotionally healthy.

When we never get back to facing our traumas, we get varied results. Because they are still inside us, they are still affecting us. This can eventually turn into physical or mental ailments as I mentioned when I discussed Dr. Bessel Van Der Kolk's book, *The Body Keeps The Score.*

> *"Trauma is not what happens to us. But what we hold*
> *inside in the absence of an empathetic witness."*
> — *Peter A Levine, PhD*

Perception Juncture

I discovered that for me it was all about being honest with myself. I had disallowed my truth for so long, I needed to discover it. That's right. You get to discover your truth now. We get to acknowledge all that we never had, all that we are leaving behind, and all that we are hoping for in the future. I have heard it said that if we don't know where we are going we won't get there but it is just as true that if we don't know where we are starting from, we won't be able to create the path to get there. Accepting all of who we are is part of that.

My negative thoughts are a part of my life. They aren't something I need to negotiate with or even fix because there is nothing wrong with me. We are not problems that need to be solved. We are not in opposition with ourselves no matter what our life looks like. Neither is our Shadow-side in opposition to us, it is full of how we view the traumas created from events that others chose for us and some that we chose for ourselves. It is a plethora of opportunities for changes we can make.

We are discovering the truth of who we really are inside and also all the pieces that were taken from us, lost, or misdirected.

Healing Our Thoughts

The thoughts that form inside our minds mainly come from our life's experiences, and when my thoughts were not managed as…they…showed…up, they progressively turned into these Demons, or limiting beliefs that controlled me and managed my life…because, well, I wasn't.

They, or rather we, can now understand that our justifications, our Demons, or limiting beliefs, are not our only reality, they are simply that, justifications. They work for us until they don't. That is when we can become the agent for ourselves that we were never allowed to be.

Balance As An Art

In his book, "The Myth of Normal," Gabor Mate discusses how we are often born with emotional toxins that have been passed to us while we were still in the womb. One of these forms comes through chemicals from an emotionally toxic mother. They can even come from her interactions with an emotionally toxic partner.

When we begin this earthly life so incredibly imbalanced, other variables like eating unhealthy foods, lack of exercise, minimal education and sleep quality will affect our overall quality of life, leading us to create havoc for ourselves and others around us if they are not addressed. It is the respectful rebalancing of our two sides that gives us the ability to not only learn to regard both sides of who we are but also to continue to micro-adjust so that we can be successful, long-term. As we use our talents, our skills and our abilities while still noticing our faults, addressing our mistakes and correcting our misunderstandings, the result becomes that balance within ourselves. We increasingly begin to see that our lives are flowing more naturally as we accept and make conscious adjustments in our choices.

Initially our actions will be flawed as we try new ways to live our lives. With more practice, we learn to interact using more grace with ourselves and others as well. It takes lots of conscious effort when we are learning something new. We eventually realize it is no longer a constant thought process because it is no longer new to our minds.

When we make the micro-adjustments needed for the two sides of our psyche, our Light-side and our Shadow-side, we find balance. Like standing, we have far greater emotional balance by continuously adjusting to the needs of both sides of ourselves as we become comfortable with who we are at our core.

Living life on purpose will still include going through the process of loss, hurt, and pain, but it will also begin to contain our recognition of joy, happiness, and love.

Looking back, my healing journey as an adult was a chaotic mess of beautiful, un-choreographed learning. It was my perfect life dance because I was learning through my own mistakes and not through someone else telling me what they thought I should do next.

Some of us may be lucky enough to have a mentor to help us on a part of our personal path, but no mentor can live our lives for us. Only we can learn what we need to live our lives our way. It can be a beautiful thing when someone else can aid our process by giving us tips and pointers, but ultimately we are the only ones who can activate those changes in our life. Our agency is the only thing that can make that happen for us.

When we use our agency, couple it with our current understanding of our Intrinsic Blueprint that is sprinkled with our creative talent seeds, our life naturally grows to become much of what we have envisioned it to be. It's not about getting to a place where everything is perfect. It's about living the process and rebalancing as life shows up, the good, the bad, the wants and the needs.

Our Incredible Selves

In her TEDx talk, "How to Stop Screwing Yourself Over," Mel Robbins mentions that the probability of being born, according to scientists, is about one in 400 trillion.

Let me say that again, the chance of you being born—as you—is one in 400 trillion! That is a very large number, and speaks to the fact that our very existence is a miracle. Countless variables needed to occur in a particular way for you to be you, and for me to be me. From egg and sperm to fertilization, and the difficulties that entails, then merging, replication, nourishment and enough space to grow into human physical life.

The process of growing inside the womb is also so much more complex than this simple explanation and there are a myriad of diverging outcomes along the way which produce vast results to make each of us fantastically unique. And that is just *before* we are born.

The complexity continues after our amazing births where life events, however they played out, had to happen in such a way to get us to the point where we could now be sitting here reading, or listening to, this book.

Are you ready to discover the awesomeness that is you?

Profound Changes

*"You learned to fight, to survive, to shut down, to keep your guard up,
to hold your breath, to expect nothing and be prepared for anything.
In this season, may you learn to breathe, laugh, sleep, dance, love,
be free, be yourself, blossom…again or for the first time."*

—Dr. Thema Bryant

My spirit animal is a cockroach. Trust me, it wasn't my first choice. I'll admit I still have trouble looking at pictures of the creatures and not feeling a bit squeamish, but I've come to find that they really are quite amazing. For instance, cockroaches tend to thrive wherever life takes them. They work in communities, creating a complex social structure. Some of them even pair up and raise their young together. They are creatures who do well in the dark where others do not, giving them major advantages. One of these advantages comes in the form of having stunning three-hundred-sixty-degree vision because their eyes consist of two thousand lenses. Even though I find them totally creepy, I think that's pretty cool.

Here's an interesting truth: some species can live a month without food. Being so resourceful, so tenacious, and so incredibly hardy, it has been widely accepted that cockroaches will likely live through Armageddon, the war that the books of the Bible describe as a last battle between good and evil and is often referred to as the end of everything—except maybe cockroaches. These insects are survivors.

Surviving Transitions

To move from surviving to living a life of your own making takes awareness and confidence to figure out what to do with new knowledge as it shows up. Throughout this book, my goal has been to create an awareness for you of your superpower, your agency. You are an individual and have never been an extension of anyone else. I've discussed how your agency still exists even when your choices are minimal. No matter what your circumstances, in every situation everyone involved plays a part in the outcome.

I also talked about your agency being distinctly personal. Because we interact with others, our lives overlap and each party makes choices that affect those around them. We only have responsibility for our actions, not the actions of others, no matter what our Demons tell us.

When we were too young, too small or too inexperienced, we depended on others to make our life decisions and the narcissist in our lives controlled our growth by creating Demons who kept us dependent on them. We went along with this because it felt safer. More than cockroaches, we are now resourceful adults with the capability to discover our own agency. We can flush out those Demon-created beliefs as we develop a life we were never allowed to have as children. When we find where we are still working from limiting beliefs in some or all areas of our lives, our agency is what gives us the power to change that.

We All Have Intrinsic Worth

My conversation with my friend, who helped me to see my intrinsic worth, was such a pivotal moment. It was where I first accepted my incredibly unique and beautiful Intrinsic Blueprint. My worth was never based on my mother's acceptance of who I was or who I would become. It was always there waiting for me to discover it. The only thing left was to decide how I was going to act for myself. Was I going to believe in my worth, now that I knew it existed, or let the Demons bring me back to that dark abyss I had once lived within?

The one thing I will say here is that it is not common to step away from our dark abyss and never again feel hopeless. Being on one side of the line or the other depends on how we choose to live long-term. Accepting that we will visit the familiar dark abyss once in a while makes it possible to pack up our things and move on. Otherwise we find ourselves stuck back there and our Demons telling us, "See? You knew it wouldn't work out. You are hopeless and nothing is going to change that."

They are liars!

Nobody is Hopeless

No, none of us are hopeless. As you learn to accept your mistakes, missteps and failings, while giving yourself grace so you can learn *from* them, you will begin to see the identifiers that will help you make the unique changes you want to make in your own life. Your changes may be different than the ones I had to make. I still make many changes and continue working on *all the things* so I can feel comfortable that my life is of my own making.

As I earlier spelled out in this chapter, I can look back and see where at each level I learned what to do next. I did not realize while I was mentally processing these lessons that I always knew what I needed to do next. With each insight I had enough realization to take steps forward, even if they were micro adjustments, until the way forward became clearer. Many of my insights came after pondering on some event that happened, deciding what I wanted to do, figuring out how to fit that into what I could actually do and acting on a first step. I usually figured things out fairly quickly but some of them took years of contemplating, and I still got some parts wrong.

It is possible for you to create something from nothing as I did. Maybe your "nothing" was far worse than mine. Your journey won't look the same, though there may be some similarities. What you and I likely have in common is abuse from a narcissistic family member that didn't look like abuse to the rest of society. The world is barely beginning to get clear on the damaging effects of narcissistic abuse.

Valuable Perceptions

But whether society views this parenting as abuse or not, how we view our traumas and what we learn through them is individually up to us. The changes you can make are within the realm of reality. No matter how long you need to take, your life can be of your own making.

As you begin to utilize your agency you will also begin to discover what that means for you, and will grow in ways you didn't realize were even possible, let alone doable. Happiness really is a possibility.

Learning to look at both your Light-side and Shadow-side with the respect and dignity you deserve, while giving yourself grace for the parts you still feel negatively about, will give you confidence until you can accept them as is or change them into what you need.

Find and embrace your Intrinsic Blueprint as the cornerstone of your core self. It can help you see more clearly how to make decisions for yourself and where to make adjustments. It will clarify your worth, that you're valuable as you are right now, and will still be valuable through any changes, any events or any traumas that ever have or ever will occur.

Your Intrinsic Blueprint can also give you transparency on what your identifiers are, and permission to do things you never before thought possible. Building on it will mean that you have stayed closer to who you are rather than trying to be something for someone else, which causes problems in a myriad of ways.

Intentional Purpose

Fighting your Demons and reaching the point where you no longer feel guilty because they exist is freedom from the bondage and slavery of the dark, life-sucking lies. No matter how well it is presented to you, if it harms you at your core, it doesn't work for you.

That said, Demons are not all bad because they are what made sense to you in the middle of a trauma that created them. Holding onto them when new information comes can be an identifier that shows you what needs to change. That may be the identifier you need to find your authenticity because identifiers give you the direction and sometimes the purpose. You now have many ways to combat them, gain your control back from them, or dismiss them when they no longer help you navigate the complexities of your traumas.

I have learned now to be grateful for the service of my Demons as I release them from the responsibilities I placed on them. I ultimately wish that for you as you navigate your Demons.

Because we are each individuals, I can't tell you how to fight your particular Demons. What I can tell you, and how I tried to write this book, is how I did it, and am still doing it, so you can take my ideas and change them to fit your style, your preferences and your personality. Maybe you, like me, have spent so much time trying to do what you see others doing and wondering why you could never feel the excitement that they seemed to be feeling. The truth is, we are not living their lives. We can only live our lives. We can only make our mistakes.

As Steve Blair said, "The best exercise is the one you will do consistently." Our Intrinsic Blueprint is the foundation of possibilities and is the basis for our own optimal happiness. Find it, learn it, continue to discover it and learn to live within your most authentic self as closely as possible. Happiness lies in who you are becoming, and as you will discover, it can also lie in who you are now even in all the mess. Maybe, after reading this book, you've started to learn this already.

Ideas For Learning About Yourself

The following are some more experiences of mine and some from friends and clients as they discovered their Demons, noticed their identifiers and what they did to utilize their Intrinsic Blueprint to find solutions that worked for them. You may find some you want to try. Please realize that some of these may not work for you so pick the ones that feel right for you. It's okay to start with only one.

Journaling

Throughout the traumas of my childhood, I journaled. As a teenager, I used small, top spiral bound notebooks that I kept in the back pocket of my jeans similar to how I now keep my phone. I would write in these notebooks whenever I felt I needed to make sense of something, complain of something or even just remember something. By the end of high school, I had over thirteen small spiral bound notebooks full of my life as I saw it. At the beginning of my college years, my fear that someone else might read them and misunderstand me led me to burn every single one of them. It was the right thing to do for me at the time but I've often wondered what it would be like to read them now; what was my perspective, and how did I view the world then? I can guess I was pretty negative since that was my go-to for just about everything back in those days. I once again write in a journal but only when I feel I have something to figure out. I've learned not to feel obligated to write in it every day. Even when I'm doing my morning pages, sometimes I go days without writing anything, and sometimes I write in it multiple times in one day. It helps me organize my thoughts.

Being With Nature

I have always lived within a city. Growing up in suburbia meant that I took to finding vacant lots, overgrown spruce trees in a yard, or even riding my bike to as many parks as I could before it got dark. As an adult, it was harder to do when my kids were little. Driving to a park, walking to a park and sitting, finding a single tree were some of the options I found useful. Taking my kids to the park was as much for me as it was for my kids. It didn't solve my problems but sometimes it gave me time to think, ponder and contemplate so I could consider whatever decision I needed to make next. Looking back, I found I was more calm when I didn't get involved with speaking with other mothers but instead actually had time to think, as long as my mind wasn't going down some rabbit hole of negativity.

Knowing I loved nature, I've often tried to have a garden. I'm not the greatest gardener but I've tried to grow various plants over the years. I've grown flowers, herbs, and I've even built two ponds. I would have to say that there have been more frustrations than yields but when I am successful it makes such a profound difference for me. The levels of positivity I feel end up outweighing the number of frustrations, so I keep trying.

Other ways I've enjoyed nature are camping, hiking, picnicking, playing with my dog, watching documentaries about nature, or just plain sitting on my porch with my bare feet on the ground. This last one doesn't happen often as my skin itches after I touch grass for too long so I usually just walk on the sidewalk barefoot as I think about the earth underneath the concrete.

My sister-in-law uses nature to work through her issues as well. She loves water and so will find streams, rivers or ponds to walk near so she can clear her head and ponder out her issues. She has discovered many Demons while pondering her disconnects on her walks.

The Beauty of Cat Napping

Taking a cat nap was something Tonya, a client friend of mine, learned to do as a young parent. I could relate. A cat nap for her was a short, usually six to fifteen-minute nap that gave her a reset to continue functioning. For her it was a power boost, and sometimes she needed a couple of them a day.

She learned to do this when her three babies were under the age of six. When they went down for a nap, she would doze with them or just lay down on the couch for a bit.

The Power of Dreams

Dreaming is a natural way our minds process our mental imbalances. Whatever we can't make sense of in our waking life, our minds try to process while we sleep. This is why sleep is considered so vitally important to our mental health. Once learning about this, I tried to focus on my dreams. I would alternate with one night choosing a focus and the next night letting my mind decide so I wasn't disrupting my brain's tendency to function naturally.

Because I was brought up by a narcissistic parent, my mind didn't understand some of the simplest things, so focusing on my old traumas with my newer understanding became a goal that I continue working on to this day. Not to judge them but to upgrade those old, worn-out beliefs.

A close friend explained how she did it this way: Start by having a notepad and pencil sitting on a table next to the bed. The last thing to do before putting your head on the pillow is to write down a one-sentence question, the simpler the better. Then Fall asleep thinking about the question.

The first thing to do upon waking is to write on the notepad whatever comes to mind no matter how strange. Don't worry about grammar, punctuation or wording. Just write. It isn't for anyone else to read.

Something else I did, but a bit harder, I utilized my dreams by actually trying to remember them. Similar to before, I would write whatever I could remember of my dreams. This worked best for me when I was processing something really big. I hadn't necessarily started with a question before bed but I would write down everything I could remember whether it made sense or not. As I collected these dreams, I began to see how some might connect. My conscious mind became privy to what my subconscious mind was trying to make sense of and I began to see how some of these linked together. The few times I was successful, I was able to figure out some details that helped me stand firm on my own and make positive decisions that mattered to me and sometimes to others close to me. This clarity helped me to make changes without harming others in the process.

Taking a Class

When I started to write this book, one of my worst Demons was the one telling me I wasn't credentialed enough to tell my story. He would consistently show me where all the people who were making a difference in this area had many letters after their name proving they knew more than me and that I was simply a wannabe. At that time I was still unsure how to stop hearing him, and no amount of positive affirmations were sufficient to dissuade the feelings that this Demon's comments created.

I was blessed with the ability to take a course to become a health coach. I now have letters after my name. Lisa Sitze MHWC, which stands for Master Health and Wellness Coach. It didn't solve the problem, I still hear the Demon screaming my incompetence at me but his words don't sting as much.

My discovery? No one is the expert on *my* life other than me, no matter how many letters they have after their name. I see education as always a good thing...at least the kind that propels us forward rather than the education we got at the hands of our abusers. That stamped down our creativity. I learned a lot through my courses but what mattered most to me was the lesson that we are the only ones who can make real, lasting changes for ourselves. Only we have the capacity to live our lives our way. No one else can do that for us.

Going For a Drive

When my mother tried to kill herself the first time, I tried to figure out my place in this new dynamic. I was so angry at her for her attempted suicide but I also knew that yelling at her about it wouldn't change her reasons for trying it. I wasn't able to hate her for her attempt at suicide but I also was unwilling to move all my attention from my small children, who needed me, to her. I found a psychologist I could relate to and would drive the forty-five minutes to get to her office once a week. Besides being a small weekly break from my parental duties, for me it also meant being able to crank my music up and sing as loud as I wanted. I found the drive more relaxing and therapeutic than the sessions with the psychologist. I had discovered a way for me to work through some of my issues that I hadn't previously been able to. After that, I kept finding reasons I had to go some place until I realized it was a necessity for me at that time. I quickly added it to my healing arsenal.

Affirmations and Declarations

Saying words enough times does make them real to your mind. It becomes even more so the more times you voice them to others, especially when intense feelings are attached. This is why affirmations and the like are so popular. The problem for us lies within our history of being raised with narcissistic abuse. The distortions became our truth.

We can still change those distortions using the same method but instead, using words of our choice. When I started this, I was told to say things I didn't believe to change my thinking. That never seemed to work for me and became one more way for my Demons to prove my incompetence.

Today I use affirmations but take it slow. If I have a goal in mind and it is currently too out of my realm of possibility, I will step it. I mean, I will figure out one step I feel I can do that will move toward that goal and use that as my affirmation until I believe that small thing. Then I will upgrade to the next step. It has not only served to help me accomplish my goals, it has pushed away the Demons that were keeping me from making goals a reality for my life.

Dancing Away the Blues

One of my best friends loves to dance. Though she didn't have narcissistic parents, she has been through some pretty difficult traumas. She spent years believing her life wasn't that bad until some events triggered her in ways she didn't realize was a problem for her. She used to go out dancing occasionally but the man she married didn't like dancing so she eventually stopped going. In the last few years, as these triggers have been infiltrating her life, she has set up a room in her home so that she could exercise, i.e., dance. I can tell the days she has danced before we do anything together, and the days she hasn't. It fills her soul.

"It's Not My Truth"

Jackson, a client of mine, who also grew up with a narcissistic parent, had a conversation with his sister that he shared with me. His sister was frustrated with him and his view of their mother as he was trying to heal from his past. In an exasperating tone, his sister asked him, "What did Mom do *right*?"

You see, his experience with their mother was vastly different from hers. When he couldn't think of anything positive to say, his sister lost it and yelled at him for almost an hour.

He and I had done enough work at that point that he knew explaining his side of the conversation was a lost cause. Jackson's sister hadn't wanted his answer. She was looking to prove *her* answers about how wonderful she thought their mother was.

Jackson told me, "It was hard to listen to her tell me all the ways she thought *I* had been the problem. In the past, I would have accepted that. After all, I'd been told that all my life. Still, I knew she only knew what Mom had said to her in their relationship—about me. My sister had little experience of our mom's darker side of which I had never been free."

He let his sister vent at him. "I wasn't going to tell her she was wrong. It was her truth." I was so impressed with this. Jackson had learned how to not take on his sister's truth simply because it wasn't his. He genuinely wanted to let her have her story while keeping his own truth intact. Even though it upset his sister, Jackson exercised his agency, and while he refused to discount her point of view, he also refused to discount his own. Not only was he willing to be authentic, he was living my very definition of safe vulnerability.

Listening vs Hearing

The other day I had a disagreement with my stepfather. We were discussing the right and wrong ways to load a dishwasher. I had one way, he had another but we both had reasons for why our way was best. Our conversation got louder and louder as we both tried to get our point across to the other person, and then I remembered something. Most people can't hear someone else's ideas until they feel heard. My stepfather wasn't feeling heard.

You see, I believe he had spent an entire life not being heard living with women, his mother and consecutively his two wives, who were either straight-up narcissists or had strong narcissistic tendencies. He was playing out his life in our current conversation. I stopped trying to make my point and began listening.

This one is hard to do when you've never been heard yourself because it is hard to get beyond your own need to be heard. As I listened, I started asking questions he could answer that gave him permission to be heard. The conversation began to be more calm and actual hearing between both of us began happening.

It was beautiful. It sounds strange to say out loud but I realized that what mattered to me was my stepfather feeling heard more than how my dishwasher got loaded. In the end, he came up with the idea that he would leave the dishes in the sink, and I would load it when I got the chance. He would then simply notice the dishwasher light to determine when it was finished and then he would unload. By simply allowing him to feel heard, he ultimately came up with a solution that we both could work with.

Progressive Acceptance

I struggled with opposite views of myself. Because I was both the golden child and the scapegoat for the first seven years of my life, I had a dual perspective of my abilities. I would go into a task (game, project, etc) knowing I could do it right and be the best. But, If things turned out different than I expected, which they often did, I would feel completely defeated and tell myself, "Of course I lost. I always lose!" I used absolutes constantly because all things seemed black and white. I had a confusing all "and" nothing attitude simultaneously.

The simplest compliment or criticism made me uncomfortable, even when I was the one saying it to myself. To heal, I started with trying to accept compliments I received, even internally, and noticing how I felt when I was criticized. It changed some perception in me and I began to wonder what others were seeing that I wasn't. I slowly began to see more things about me that I actually liked. I became better able to hear criticisms with curiosity rather than being afraid of them and outright rejecting them.

I came to realize that I needed to be the best at everything, even if I was doing it for the first time. I thought people would like me if I was the best. Now I can be happy with other people winning or having the best ideas, being happy for them while still being satisfied with my results.

I think this part took the longest. I finally began to notice that I was actually happy for someone else's success without feeling like I had messed up somehow, like I wasn't good enough. It was a wonderful freeing feeling to be sure. I first learned to be okay with how long it took me to learn this regardless of the lies my Demons were telling me like, I should have figured this out long ago.

Using affirmations, my steps went something like this.

I'm satisfied with the way I am, (This took about a month.)

I'm okay with the way I am, (This took close to a year.)

I accept the way I am, (This took a couple of months.)

I am happy with the way I am, (This took a few years. I still come back to it occasionally.)

I embrace the way I am. (This one comes and goes as I learn to keep it as my truth. For me, it must include balancing my responsibility for the part I play in how I affect mine and others' lives.)

This process took years for me to complete, and it is still ongoing. Some of us have to step towards positive feelings to embrace the way we are.

Lessons of Living Alone

My maternal grandmother lived alone as long as I knew her. She was always old to me. I saw her as someone who was going to die anytime but leave this world busy. Shortly after I graduated from basic camp, I went to stay with her for a couple of months. We went all over her area in upstate New York, visiting and doing community work. I have memories of her completely rebuilding the cabinets in the rental home she lived in when she was in her late sixties, traveling the state to visit sick friends, and writing eleven family name biographies. She wanted them to read like novels so when you began reading, you would have a hard time putting each book down. She also kept up with four different soap operas. In her earlier years, she was a stock car racer and had her name included in the Dirt Motorsports Hall of Fame. I still have a pic of her plaque.

During my visits with her, she taught me all sorts of things but the biggest ones I remember were her comments about living alone. "When you live alone, you don't have to work around anyone else's schedule. You don't have to worry about people moving your stuff. You don't have to wait for the bathroom. You also don't have anyone to talk to when you need companionship, and there is no one to blame when something is misplaced. Having full access to the bathroom is always a plus."

When It's Time for Your New Chapter

I t is the discovery of your superpower that can propel self-work forward faster than anything else. Even if it takes a while to realize, you always have the power to choose the way you live your life. When you didn't know or understand this power, you only had old, false beliefs to make decisions upon, many of which you were taught. This gave you agency with a horrific, nuclear half-life. It isn't true agency because you were not safe to make choices outside your narcissistic parents' dictates. Even after you left home, those teachings followed you like a life-sucking parasite.

For me, my trauma bond with my mother kept me from allowing myself to recognize my own agency. Now, you and I have the potential to look back and feel hopeful rather than helpless. We no longer need to be who we were, who they molded us to be.

- We can learn to see the lies our narcissistic parents' presented as truths.
- We can recognize the needs that were not filled by our caretakers and find our own healthy ways to fill them.
- We can learn to give ourselves grace for mistakes we make along our healing journey.
- We can learn the confidence to create boundaries with ourselves and allow ourselves to create boundaries with others, no matter how long it takes us.

- We can notice the identifiers that show us our limiting beliefs because our boundaries are being crossed, ignored, or downright obliterated, sometimes by us.
- We can practice our own life balance, creating more steadiness as we acknowledge and accept where we are so we can get to where we want to be.
- When we have times of struggle, like all humans, we can search for and look to our Intrinsic Blueprint to guide us because it is *us*—at our most core self that contains our true potential.

The true gift, then, the deeper component, is being able to make choices about it all—how we feel about our experiences, how we see our childhood, and what we do with any identifiers as they show up. All this takes time to practice as we process them.

The most exciting thing is that now that you know what to look for, and as you learn to be more honest with yourself about your thoughts and your actions, you will have the opportunity to make the changes you may have never been allowed—nor been able to give yourself permission to make. Equally motivating is the knowledge that when you struggle (like all humans), you now have the possibility to use your Intrinsic Blueprint to guide you in figuring out your part as it is your foundation, your core.

I'd like to be clear. You may never personally see a diagnosis about a parent with narcissism. The great news is that you don't necessarily need that to learn that your childhood dissociations were outside of your control. You now have the tools to notice the identifiers so you can recognize your needs that were not met as you were growing up. Through all your experiences, though it was hidden from you, your new awareness of your agency grants you this ability to live your life your way, not someone else's way.

As you discover your own Intrinsic Blueprint, you will find an authentic place inside of yourself that helps you make decisions uniquely right for you and helps you create your boundaries for yourself and how others interact with you. It will help you make the decisions that will be uniquely right for you. This one is yours. And…it really is okay if what works for you doesn't fully work for others. It allows you the ability to live your life purpose. Give yourself time to learn what that means for you.

My one personal truth that kept me grounded was that God existed and loved me unconditionally. Even though my mother told me, "God can't exist because too many bad things happen to good people," I kept coming back to my own personal belief throughout each of my small steps. It was a truth I felt at my core. After learning about his gifting all of us our agency, his own understanding of the lessons I would learn as I went through my experiences has been my most significant realization.

I only brought God into the conversation here for a reason. Although he was a major part of *my* healing journey, for me, his most remarkable contribution was giving me the freedom to learn the lessons. The experiences I went through before I was old enough to understand life were the start of the gifts that gave me the secret sauce to create my life, my way. I feel like God let me do this. I feel he led me along, helping me to become greater for my trials instead of weaker. I feel he was always there watching over me.

Whether you believe in God, a higher power, or any other form of "bigger than you" potential, now that you know, your agency is yours to learn to consciously control. There are so many ways we experience and grow in this life, but the biggest growth happens when we are the ones who make our life happen for ourselves. Facing your Demons is a great act of self-love. Even if all you do is change your thinking from what your narcissistic parent forced you to think, each of those Demons you recognize reveals your identifiers. Every time you use these identifiers to make the changes you need, your life becomes a bit more authentic, a bit more powerful, a bit more *safe*…until you become more comfortable in your own skin.

Your own Intrinsic Blueprint helps you create your own unique solutions.

I will say it again, it really *is* okay if it doesn't work for others. No one has been through exactly what you have. God can only do so much if he is going to let us grow. He knows we must be the ones to give ourselves time to learn what our experiences mean for our lives.

Our brilliant survival skills that were learned under gaslighting, constant criticism, or maybe even physical or sexual abuse helped us survive. We may not have had safety growing up, but we can design that safety in the life we create for ourselves today.

At the end of the day, the vital question becomes: now that you have been given a glimpse into your agency, what will you do with your superpower?

My Glossary
of Definitions

I am including a list of terms I use and the meaning with which I use them in my book. I am not changing the meanings of words but I have introduced a few words that are not typically used. To keep what I'm saying easier to understand, I am defining them in this glossary.

Agency: Agency is the capacity to act and learn from our own experiences because it is the privilege for us to choose how we act for ourselves and not to be acted upon. Agency is not the same as freedom.

Apartheid: (In South Africa) a policy or system of segregation or discrimination on grounds of race.

Authenticity: (Oxford Online Dictionary) The quality of being real or true. I would add that being true to oneself will change as one grows, learns and expands one's knowledge. (From the online APA Dictionary of Psychology) A mode of being that humans can achieve by accepting the burden of freedom, choice, and responsibility and the need to construct their own values and meanings in a meaningless universe. —authentic *adj.*

Balance: Taking into account both our Light–side *and* our Shadow–side as having value and worth for our circumstances. (From the online APA Dictionary of Psychology) A harmonious relationship or equilibrium of opposing forces or contrasting elements.

Balanced: Acting without malice, guilt or anger, which includes viewing ourselves without condemnation or judgment, noticing—when our Light-side and Shadow-side are balanced equally, we are living our truth at our core.

Complex Post Traumatic Stress Disorder (CPTSD): (See also PTSD) (Note: This term is not in the DSM-5. Because many of the psychologists and psychiatrists I have asked to help me seem to understand this term themselves and acknowledged it as a valid term, so I am including it here in my glossary.)

(Cleveland Clinic – (Complex PTSD)) Complex post-traumatic stress disorder (Complex PTSD) can result from experiencing chronic trauma, such as prolonged child abuse or domestic violence. It's closely related to PTSD and borderline personality disorder.

(PubMed) Individuals with complex PTSD typically have sustained multiple exposures to trauma, such as childhood abuse and domestic or community violence.

Also see: Post Traumatic Stress Disorder.

Constructed Identities: Identities we take on because of our own mix of nature vs nurture. Similar to masking and functions alongside the masks we wear.

Core: The epitome of who we are and the place where our principles can be found despite what has happened to us in our lives. The center of our whole being. (Oxford Language Dictionary) The central or most important part of something. The core is the essence of our spirit and the true character or foundation of our individual soul, bowels.

Covert Narcissism: Also called vulnerable narcissism. This term refers to narcissistic personality traits that are not readily apparent. Grandiose, secret, life done them wrong, passive-aggressive, hyper-sensitive to criticism, fear of abandonment, and characterized by a person's tendency to mask their narcissistic traits.

Psychology Today – Understanding Covert Narcissism

Demons: Limiting Beliefs created during traumas, major confusions, misconceptions, or lack of ability. They temporarily serve us until our circumstances change, and then they become detrimental because they can't learn or grow, they stay the same age as we were when we created them; they become multi-layered when used long-term; triggers will incite them anew.

Disconnect: The mental disconnect one experiences from the world around them when their caretaker has Narcissistic Personality Disorder. Emotional detachment. Sometimes called dissociation. (From the online APA Dictionary of Psychology) A defense mechanism in which conflicting impulses are kept apart or threatening ideas and feelings are separated from the rest of the psyche.

Dissociated State: (APA Dictionary of Psychology) A reaction to a traumatic event in which the individual splits the components of the event into those that can be faced in the present and those that are too harmful to process.

Emotion Regulation: (APA Dictionary of Psychology – Emotion Regulation) (https://dictionary.apa.org/emotion-regulation:

Emotion regulation is taught to children by their parents by letting them feel their feelings. This ability to modulate an emotion or set of emotions is called emotion regulation. Straightforward emotion regulation needs conscious monitoring which can entail learning to see situations in multiple ways so as to better manage the feelings created by them. It can also require changing the focus of the presented emotion, like fear or anger, to end on more positive results.

"Implicit emotion regulation operates without deliberate monitoring; it modulates the intensity or duration of an emotional response without the need for awareness. Emotion regulation typically increases across the lifespan."

Emotional Intelligence: (APA Dictionary of Psychology – Emotional Intelligence) https://dictionary.apa.org/emotional-intelligence

A type of intelligence that involves the ability to process emotional information and use it in reasoning and other cognitive activities, proposed by U.S. psychologists Peter Salovey (1958–) and John D. Mayer (1953–). According to Mayer and Salovey's 1997 model, it comprises four abilities: to perceive and appraise emotions accurately; to access and evoke emotions when they facilitate cognition; to comprehend emotional language and make use of emotional information; and to regulate one's own and others' emotions to promote growth and well-being.

Flooded: An opiate-induced state of fight, flight, freeze or faint. It naturally blinds us to our agency, and we react rather than act with intention. Of itself, I feel it is neutral and can be helpful like when running from a tiger, or hurtful, like when lashing out at loved ones unfairly.

Freedom: (Oxford Language Dictionary) The power or right to act, speak, or think as one wants without hindrance or restraint.

Gaslighting: (APA Dictionary of Psychology – Gaslight) *vb.* To manipulate another person into doubting their perceptions, experiences, or understanding of events. The term once referred to manipulation so extreme as to induce mental illness or to justify commitment of the gaslighted person to a psychiatric institution but is now used more generally. It is usually considered a colloquialism, though occasionally it is seen in clinical literature, referring, for example, to the manipulative tactics associated with antisocial personality disorder (https://dictionary.apa.org/gaslight).

(Psychology Today) "Gaslighting is an insidious form of manipulation and psychological control. Victims of gaslighting are deliberately and systematically fed false information that leads them to question what they know to be true, too often about themselves. They may end up doubting their memory, their perception, and even their sanity. Over time, a gaslighter's manipulations can grow more complex and potent, making it increasingly difficult for the victim to see the truth."

—gaslighted *adj.* [from Gaslight, a 1938 stage play and two later film adaptations (1940, 1944) in which a wife is nearly driven to insanity by the deceptions of her husband]

Grace: To show courtesy for mistakes and faults in oneself and others.

Humbly Confident: standing fully in your own authenticity while respecting the agency of others, being able to respect the choices of others and where they are in their life journey while standing up for your own choices, being able to make your own life choices that may or may not affect others.

Identifiers: Identifiers expose our limiting potential. They may have become invisible to our abuse-trained minds to keep us safe from more abuse. They show up throughout our lives to make our traumas clearer to our understanding so we can work through them. They can show up as shadows in what we thought was empty space in our mind. Identifiers are not triggers, though, triggers could be identifiers.

Influences: Religion, parent, past traumas, family, friends, genetics, stop signs, the weather, happy memories, bad memories, our thoughts, our emotions, our culture, our attitude, our beliefs, distractions, Demons, potentially anything and everything.

Integrity: (Oxford Dictionary) The quality of being honest and having strong moral principles; moral uprightness. [I personally believe strongly that the moral principles in this definition should include being respectful and honoring the agency of everyone.]

Intrinsic: (Merriam-Webster Dictionary) Belonging to the essential nature or constitution of a thing.

Intrinsic Blueprint: The foundation of our life purpose; who we are at our most authentic self, from which, if we build upon, will bring into being a life where we feel most fulfilled. It contains everything we might need, like our natural talents, to fulfill that life purpose. It also contains seeds for us to nurture and expand our life purpose as we grow more talents. Our Intrinsic Blueprint runs solely on our agency. Though it can be hidden from us or made more difficult to utilize, it cannot be messed up or taken away by others. It also cannot be destroyed by anything that happens to us in our lives.

Light-side: Working space for our conscious beliefs and understandings: successes, triumphs, understandings, our truth. It also is where we consciously work on traumas that we had hidden from ourselves previously and are ready to work through them.

Masks: At the time of me writing this book, the only form of masking was primarily used in reference to Autism and ADHD. Though it is recognized in these areas in the psychology world, I haven't found a direct reference to narcissistic abuse but I have talked to many psychologists who do feel this abuse creates masking due to the nature of the abuse. Masks are something almost everyone wears for various reasons. I will give my own definition related to narcissistic abuse specifically.

Masking is what a person shows the world when what is underneath is mental turmoil. Masks can be worn by the abused and also the abuser. In the case of NPD, the narcissist wears one to show the world how perfect they are. Those abused by a narcissist wear one to protect themselves from the narcissist's wrath should anyone find out that their abuser or their home life is less than perfect.

Mindset: The beliefs at the conscious and subconscious level that determine how we act and feel. (Oxford Language Dictionary) The established set of attitudes held by someone.

Narcissism: (Dr. Ramani: American Clinical Psychologist) A noun, a descriptive term that captures a pattern characterized by a rigid, maladaptive, antagonistic personality style.

Narcissistic Personality Disorder: (Psychology Today) Two types: grandiose (overt) marked by extroversion, self-confidence, attention seeking, and aggression. Vulnerable (covert) characterized by introversion, high sensitivity, negative emotions and a need for constant recognition and reassurance. A unifying theme of all forms of narcissistic personality disorder is self-enhancement, the belief that one's thoughts and actions set them apart from others. (APA Dictionary of Psychology) A personality disorder with the following characteristics: (a) a long-standing pattern of grandiose self-importance and an exaggerated sense of talent and achievements; (b) fantasies of unlimited sex, power, brilliance, or beauty; (c) an exhibitionistic need for attention and admiration; (d) either cool indifference or feelings of rage, humiliation, or emptiness as a response to criticism, indifference, or defeat; and (e) various interpersonal disturbances, such as feeling entitled to special favors, taking advantage of others, and inability to empathize with the feelings of others, included in DSM-IV-TR, DSM-5, and DSM-5-TR. [originally formulated by psychoanalysts Wilhelm Reich (1897-1957), Otto Kernberg (1928-), and Heinz Kohut (1913-1981) and psychologist Theodore Millon]

Overcoming: To move beyond the anger, bitterness and resentment and no longer be triggered beyond the ability to act for oneself. No longer reacting to the pain caused by the trauma of narcissistic abuse but instead acting with more positive intention for your life. There can still be anger, resentment and bitterness, but it no longer runs you.

Perfect: Optimal for the situation.

Personal Armageddon: A Personal Armageddon is a life crisis. It is reaching the end of your rope for coping with what is happening in your life. Though we each have different levels of coping abilities, our Personal Armageddon is us reaching the point where we can no longer pretend to live in that forced inauthenticity. It is a mental breakdown that creates a complete and total desire to change your circumstances.

Personality Disorder: (National Institutes of Health) A deeply ingrained pattern of behavior of a specified kind that deviates markedly from the norms of generally accepted behavior, typically apparent by the time of adolescence, and causing long-term difficulties in personal relationships in society. (APA Dictionary of Psychology; any in a group of disorders involving pervasive patterns of perceiving, relating to, and thinking about the environment and the self that interfere with long-term functioning of the individual and are not limited to isolated episodes.)

Post Traumatic Stress Disorder (PTSD): (See also Complex PTSD) (Mayo-clinic) A mental health condition that's triggered by a terrifying event—either experiencing it or witnessing it.

(American Psychiatric Association – What is Post Traumatic Stress Disorder (PTSD)?) A psychiatric disorder that may occur in people who have experienced or witnessed a traumatic event, series of events or set of circumstances. An individual may experience this as emotionally or physically harmful or life-threatening and may affect mental, physical, social, and/or spiritual well-being.

Power: Our agency. (APA Dictionary of Psychology) The capacity to influence others, even when they try to resist this influence.

Principles: (Stephen Covey) External rules that are permanent and unchanging. (Oxford Language Dictionary) A fundamental truth or proposition that serves as the foundation for a system of belief or behavior or for a chain of reasoning.

[Note: Because I use the term safety so often in this book, I felt it rather important that I define it here. Unfortunately, the term safety is mostly used to mean in the workplace. Although that is valuable, those definitions don't work here. The safety I'm speaking of in this book is more about 'psychological safety' which was coined by the psychologist and psychotherapist Carl Rogers in 1950 to establish the conditions necessary to foster an individual's creativity. (Psychological safety reference: psycnet.apa.org – The role of psychological safety in human development) https://psycnet.apa.org/record/2016-12248-002)

I will write my interpretations here.

Safety definition 1 (temporary safety): Respite from the pain caused by abuse or trauma.

Safety definition 2: Freedom from the hypervigilant fear of impending doom stemming from painful, hurtful or abusive interactions with authority figures.

(Oxford Language Dictionary): The condition of being protected from or unlikely to cause danger, risk, or injury.

Safe-vulnerability: Feeling safe enough to be wrong, make mistakes or mess up while staying in authenticity, allowing others to be where they are in their growth while still keeping yourself safe from any perceived abuse.

Self-actualization: (Maslow) The highest level of psychological development, where personal potential is fully realized after basic bodily and ego needs have been fulfilled. Also called self-realization. (APA Dictionary of Psychology) The complete realization of that of which one is capable, involving maximum development of abilities and full involvement in and appreciation for life, particularly as it manifests in peak experiences.

Shadow Self: (Carl Jung) The shadow is a living part of the personality, and therefore wants to live with it in some form. It cannot be argued out of existence or rationalized into harmlessness. This problem is exceedingly difficult, because it not only challenges the whole man, but reminds him at the same time of his helplessness and ineffectuality.

Shadow-Side: Holding place for past traumas as things too difficult for our psyche to understand when they happened. It contains our mistakes we won't accept, our faults we disregard, our misunderstandings and things we refuse to believe about our true selves.

Stewardship: (Marriam-Webster Dictionary) The conducting, supervising, or managing of something, especially the careful and responsible management of something entrusted to one's care. My personal idea of stewardship is watching over the welfare of someone while respecting your charge's growth process as you guide, not force, them at their chosen pace (not yours).

Trauma: (APA Dictionary of Psychology) Any disturbing experience that results in significant fear, helplessness, dissociation, confusion, or other disruptive feelings intense enough to have a long-lasting negative effect on a person's attitudes, behavior, and other aspects of functioning. Traumatic events include those caused by human behavior (e.g., rape, war, industrial accidents) as well as by nature (i.g., earthquakes, hurricanes), and often challenge an individual's view of the world as a just, safe, and predictable place.

Trauma Bonding: When a person forms a deep emotional connection to an abuser. It is a somatic addiction to the abuser despite awareness of the abuse. (Psychology Today) Trauma-bonding is a hormonal attachment created by repeated abuse, sprinkled with being "saved" every now and then. This happens because the body's threat response (fight, flight, freeze, fawn) turns off the part of the brain that can think long-term when we are in crisis. This creates the feeling that we need the abuser to survive, and is often mistaken for "love."

Traits: (Oxford Language Dictionary) A distinguishing quality or characteristic, typically one belonging to a person. (APA Dictionary of Psychology) An enduring personality characteristic that describes or determines an individual's behavior across a range of situations.

Triggers: Anything that unexpectedly provokes intense emotions. They are usually connected to a traumatic event. Details can often be brought back to the conscious mind. This can also be viewed as an awakening of something being amiss, and can be an identifier.

Triggered (neutral): Stimuli in one's body that something is potentially dangerous or exciting

Value/s: (Stephen Covey) Internal and subjective so may change over time. (APA Dictionary of Psychology) A moral, social, or aesthetic principle accepted by an individual or society as a guide to what is good, desirable, or important.

(What I thought value meant) Having a place in society because you are needed.

(What I've learned it means) My interpretation of how I can be a benefit in my society.

Worth: (APA Dictionary of Psychology) An individual's evaluation of themselves as a valuable, capable human being deserving of respect and consideration.

Additional Resources

These links in this resource section were active and live at the time this book was published.

Introduction:

Trauma Bond definition (Cleveland Clinic: Here's What Trauma Bonding Really is and How to Recognize the Signs)
https://health.clevelandclinic.org/trauma-bonding

American Psychiatric Association: (Psychiatry.org: What is Narcissistic Personality Disorder?)
https://www.psychiatry.org/News-room/APA-Blogs/What-Is-Narcissistic-Personality-Disorder

DSM5 – PDF (pg 669-672)
https://repository.poltekkes-kaltim.ac.id/657/1/Diagnostic%20and%20statistical%20manual%20of%20mental%20disorders%20_%20DSM-5%20(%20PDFDrive.com%20).pdf

APA Dictionary of Psychology: (dictionary.apa.org – narcissistic personality disorder)
https://dictionary.apa.org/narcissistic-personality-disorder

Definition of Narcissistic Personality Disorder from the DSM 5 (psycnet.apa.org – Narcissistic personality disorder in DSM-5)
https://psycnet.apa.org/doiLanding?doi=10.1037%2Fper0000023

Narcissistic Personality Disorder (Mayoclinic.org – narcissistic personality disorder)

https://www.mayoclinic.org/diseases-conditions/narcissistic-personality-disorder/symptoms-causes/syc-20366662

https://www.psychiatry.org/news-room/apa-blogs/what-is-narcissistic-personality-disorder

Newport Institute article: How Having a Narcissistic Parent Affects Young Adult Mental Health

https://www.newportinstitute.com/resources/mental-health/narcissistic-parent/

Chapter 1:

Using the term Narcissistic vs Narcissism: Narcissism is NOT a diagnosis (DoctorRamani YouTube – Narcissism is not a diagnosis) https://www.youtube.com/watch?v=q0OHXUb4vqM&ab_channel=DoctorRamani

Who is Carl Jung (CarlJung.co – about Carl Jung) http://www.carljung.co/about-carl-jung/

Chapter 2:

Kirk Duncan: (3keyelements.com – Kirk Duncan) https://3keyelements.com/kirk-duncan/

Lao-tzu (Laozi-Chinese Daoist philosopher):

Encyclopedia Britannica: (Britannica.com – Laozi) https://www.britannica.com/biography/Laozi

Internet Encyclopedia of Philosophy: (iep.utm.edu – Laozi) *(https://iep.utm.edu/laozi/)

Chapter 3:

Links about Abraham Maslow:
(pbs.org – Abraham Maslow)
Books and Publications by and about Maslow: (maslow.com) http://www.maslow.com/

Chapter 4:

Nelson Mandela Foundation: (nelsonmandela.org)
https://www.nelsonmandela.org/
History.com Nelson Mandela: (history.com – Nelson Mandela)
*(https://www.history.com/topics/africa/nelson-mandela)
*Movies about Mandela:
*Nelson Mandela: Beyond the Myth: https://www.youtube.com/watch?v=Yn9qtrNzOyM
*Mandela: Son of Africa, Father of a Nation pts 1 & 2: https://www.youtube.com/watch?v=XPSt6oUDL6s
*Nelson Mandela: Madiba: https://www.youtube.com/watch?v=EfCoyu7m4a4
Harvard Business Review: What Breaking the 4-Minute Mile Taught us About the Limits of Conventional Thinking: (hbe.org – What Breaking the 4-Minute Mile Taught us About the Limits of Conventional Thinking) https://hbr.org/2018/03/what-breaking-the-4-minute-mile-taught-us-about-the-limits-of-conventional-thinking
Guinness World Records (guinnessworldrecords.com – first sub four minute mile)
https://www.guinnessworldrecords.com/records/hall-of-fame/first-sub-four-minute-mile#:~:text=HomeRecordsHall%20of%20Fame,Tap%20to%20unmute

*BBC Archive video: (youtube.com – 1954: Roger Bannister runs the first ever 4 minute mile) https://www.youtube.com/watch?v=Nb5AtK08gPM

National Library of Medicine (From Chemistry to Circuitry): https://www.ncbi.nlm.nih.gov/books/NBK234149/

Chapter 5:

About Dr. Ronald Fairbairn; (Psychoanalysis.org – Ronald Fairbairn) https://psychoanalysis.org.uk/our-authors-and-theorists/ronald-fairbairn

Chapter 6:

Peter Salovey and John D. Mayer (March 1990) "Emotional Intelligence" Sage Journals, Imagination, Cognition and Personality, Volume 9, Issue 3
https://journals.sagepub.com/doi/abs/10.2190/DUGG-P24E-52WK-6CDG#core-collateral-info

How emotional intelligence emerged. (American Psychological Association; APA.org – How Emotional Intelligence Emerged)
https://www.apa.org/monitor/oct03/emotional

A Theory of Human Motivation by Abraham Maslow: (psychclassics – A Theory of Human Motivation by Abraham Maslow)
https://psychclassics.yorku.ca/Maslow/motivation.htm

*Gabor Mate in conversation with Tara Westover: The Myth of Normal: (YouTube)
https://www.youtube.com/watch?v=UOrE7N7FGf0

*Somatic Experiencing with Michele Lee Nieves
(micheleleenieves.com – somatic experiencing)
https://www.micheleleenieves.com/somatic-experiencing

*__Mel Robins TedX talk__, "How to stop screwing yourself over" (YouTube)

https://www.youtube.com/watch?v=Lp7E973zozc&t=2s

Chapter 7:

*__Cockroach Symbolism__ (spirit-animals.com – cockroach symbolism)
https://www.spirit-animals.com/cockroach-symbolism/
__American Museum of Natural History website;__ (amnh.org – For Your Consideration: The Incredible...Roach)
https://www.amnh.org/explore/videos/biodiversity/cockroach-ecosystem

__General Links for more study:__
__DSM-5 purchase:__ https://www.psychiatry.org/psychiatrists/practice/dsm
__American Psychiatric Association:__ https://www.psychiatry.org/
__Mayo Clinic:__ https://www.mayoclinic.org/
*__Dr. Ramani, American Clinical Psychologist:__
https://www.youtube.com/@DoctorRamani

__A fun read:__
*__History of Narcissistic Personality Disorder__ (verywellmind.com – the history of narcissistic personality disorder)
https://www.verywellmind.com/the-history-of-narcissistic-personality-disorder-2795569#citation-2

Book Bibliography

The Seven Habits of Highly Effective People by Steven Covey
Man's Search For Meaning by Viktor Frankl
The Body Keeps the Score: Brain, Mind and Body in the Healing of Trauma by Bessel Van Der Kolk
It's Just My Nature by Carol Tuttle
The Artist's Way: A Spiritual Path to Higher Creativity by Julia Cameron
Wanting by Luke Bergis
But It's Your Family…Cutting Ties with Toxic Family Members and Loving Yourself in the Aftermath by Dr. Sherrie Campbell
The Myth of Normal: Trauma, Illness and Healing in a Toxic Culture by Gabor Mate

Acknowledgments

Bridget Cook Burch – for helping guide me to write my own book.

Kirk Duncan – for helping me learn to balance self-respect with my respect for others

Melody Sitze – for being my best friend even when I was struggling through my most darkest times.

Wendy Bowers, Carmel Clark, Jeanie Cisco Meth and others – for teaching me how to allow my book to be written and helping me learn to set my boundaries.

My children – for putting up with and sticking with me through your whole lives. I'm grateful you are willing to actively keep me in your lives!

Dr. Ramani and also Michele Lee Nieves – for giving me safe spaces to learn that I'm not alone or crazy.

Katie McKay – for helping me develop the words on the page for clarity in content and flow. You were an amazing help to me!

My husband – for supporting me financially and being willing to learn to allow me to hide for days while still letting me know I am not alone.

To more friends, neighbors, and acquaintances than I have room to acknowledge. You know who you are!

And every amazing person on my publishing team. You rock!

About the Author

Lisa is a writer, mother of five grown children and granny to seven grandchildren. Her favorite hobbies are playing Enshrouded, exercising, sewing, and gardening. She homeschooled her five children for sixteen years and ran a successful homeschool group for three of those years.

She has been life coaching since 2021, being certified through Dr. Sears Wellness Institute. Lisa's individualized program, to help people do deep dives into themselves, teaches clients how it is possible to use their agency to create their life their way while still respectfully balancing the needs of others.

Learn more about Lisa at *Facingyourdemonsbook.com*.
Follow/Connect with Lisa: *FacingYourDemonsbook@gmail.com*

Reviews

"Lisa's candid account of her journey is a true inspiration for those of us raised by narcissists. Her story is heartfelt, relatable, and informative. This well-written book provides valuable insights and encouragement for anyone navigating similar challenges. I highly recommend purchasing this book and joining her on this transformative journey."

—**Madison Frederick,** Best-Selling Author of Untangle the Web of Narcissism

"As someone who has also survived growing up with narcissistic relationships, I have never felt more seen or understood as I have with reading this book. Here are a few quotes that made me feel most seen while reading:

"As children, we looked to our parents as god-like and their reality as global truth."

"All is not lost! Believe it or not, triggers can be helpful if we can learn to see them as simply reminders of issues we have not yet fully worked through."

"Those of us who grew up with one or more narcissistic parents may have often been denied our childhood needs if they were inconvenient to our parent."

It is relieving to take back some power after reading this while also feeling even more so like I belong—belong to myself, belong to my world, belong to my hopes, my dreams, and aspirations. Thank you for your vulnerability and your truth."

—**Mercy Morant**

"Lisa shares intentionally facing her demons of past trauma, acknowledging and addressing hurt inflicted by a parent responsible for loving, protecting and guiding her. Determined to break an unpleasant cycle, she perseveres; providing suggested strategies utilized to prevent being defined by the effects of atrocities. She encourages identifying your "Blueprint" to live your full potential, striving daily to become better. She warns of fluctuating efforts, but sees the rewards. You can't change the past or how people relate to you, but could make firm decisions that bring joyous gains, taking control, living life your way, embracing God's unconditional love."

—**Natasha R McCoy,** #1 International Best Selling Author, Speaker, Bible Instructor. Email: natashamccoynovels@gmail.com

"I appreciate Lisa's vulnerability in sharing her story, and the modalities of healing that have worked for her. I especially value her words about Boundaries because that is where I am in my own healing journey. Naming and acknowledging our Demons is half the battle won, in my opinion, and there are many resources and people who can help us navigate the impact of those Demons. The message of this book is a monumental step in helping us do just that."

—**Angela M Walters,** PHom

"It was a joy to read your book. I want to go back and do another "Deep Dive" of your book because it has so many beautiful thoughts and tools, and integrates much more psychology than my experience with a therapist.

From the culmination of a lifetime of experience, Sitze not only shares her journey with her readers in her book Facing Your Demons, she shares it from an expert's perspective, complete with an analysis of the psychological effects of Narcissism on both the tender formative childhood years and into adulthood. She identifies and breaks down the psychology behind the confusing behaviors of both the Narcissist and their prey, providing clarity to the whirlwind of confusion caused by emotional trauma and inner demons that plague the victim.

Sitze brings with her all her knowledge from coaching others through their demons and includes Deep Dive reflections for her readers to meditate and become more cognizant of their own placement within their personal journey. She guides the reader through the healing process, giving them understanding, clarity and tools to reclaim their agency, reshape their lives and discover their true identity, setting them on the path to achieve self-actualization."

—**Salena Hamberlin,** Clinical Speech-Language Pathologist and Adjunct Professor at Texas A&M University-Kingsville

"In Facing Your Demons: Healing Beyond Narcissistic Family Relationships, Lisa Sitze delivers a raw and heartfelt exploration of growing up with a narcissistic mother. Through her courageous journey to healing, she shares practical tools and guidance to help others navigate their own recovery. This powerful book offers transformative insights that go beyond narcissistic abuse, empowering readers to take control of their lives, embrace their agency, and create a life of beauty and fulfillment—no matter their past."

—**Michelle Reittinger,** Bipolar Recovery Coach, #1 International Bestselling Author, Speaker, Coach

www.ingramcontent.com/pod-product-compliance
Lightning Source LLC
Chambersburg PA
CBHW021151130626
46554CB00005B/1765